John Farnham's Whispering Jack

33 1/3 Global

33 1/3 Global, a series related to but independent from **33 1/3**, takes the format of the original series of short, music-based books and brings the focus to music throughout the world. With initial volumes focusing on Japanese and Brazilian music, the series will also include volumes on the popular music of Australia/Oceania, Europe, Africa, the Middle East, and more.

33 1/3 Japan

Series Editor: Noriko Manabe

Spanning a range of artists and genres – from the 1970s rock of Happy End to technopop band Yellow Magic Orchestra, the Shibuya-kei of Cornelius, classic anime series *Cowboy Bebop,* J-Pop/EDM hybrid Perfume, and vocaloid star Hatsune Miku – **33 1/3 Japan** is a series devoted to in-depth examination of Japanese popular music of the twentieth and twenty-first centuries.

Published Titles:
Supercell's *Supercell* by Keisuke Yamada
Yoko Kanno's *Cowboy Bebop Soundtrack* by Rose Bridges
Perfume's *Game* by Patrick St. Michel
Cornelius's *Fantasma* by Martin Roberts
Joe Hisaishi's *My Neighbor Totoro: Soundtrack* by Kunio Hara
Shonen Knife's *Happy Hour* by Brooke McCorkle
Nenes' *Koza Dabasa* by Henry Johnson

Forthcoming Titles:
Yuming's *The 14th Moon* by Lasse Lehtonen
Yellow Magic Orchestra's *Yellow Magic Orchestra* by Toshiyuki Ohwada
Kohaku utagassen: The Red and White Song Contest by Shelley Brunt

33 1/3 Brazil

Series Editor: Jason Stanyek

Covering the genres of samba, tropicália, rock, hip hop, forró, bossa nova, heavy metal and funk, among others, **33 1/3 Brazil** is a series devoted to in-depth examination of the most important Brazilian albums of the twentieth and twenty-first centuries.

Published Titles:

Caetano Veloso's *A Foreign Sound* by Barbara Browning

Tim Maia's *Tim Maia Racional Vols. 1 &2* by Allen Thayer

João Gilberto and Stan Getz's *Getz/Gilberto* by Brian McCann

Gilberto Gil's *Refazenda* by Marc A. Hertzman

Dona Ivone Lara's *Sorriso Negro* by Mila Burns

Milton Nascimento and Lô Borges's *The Corner Club* by Jonathon Grasse

Racionais MCs' *Sobrevivendo no Inferno* by Derek Pardue

Naná Vasconcelos's *Saudades* by Daniel B. Sharp

Forthcoming titles:

Jorge Ben Jor's *África Brasil* by Frederick J. Moehn

Chico Buarque's *Chico Buarque* by Charles A. Perrone

33 1/3 Europe

Series Editor: Fabian Holt

Spanning a range of artists and genres, **33 1/3 Europe** offers engaging accounts of popular and culturally significant albums of Continental Europe and the North Atlantic from the twentieth and twenty-first centuries.

Published Titles:

Darkthrone's *A Blaze in the Northern Sky* by Ross Hagen

Ivo Papazov's *Balkanology* by Carol Silverman

Heiner Müller and Heiner Goebbels's *Wolokolamsker Chaussee* by
    Philip V. Bohlman

Modeselektor's *Happy Birthday!* by Sean Nye

Mercyful Fate's *Don't Break the Oath* by Henrik Marstal

Bea Playa's *I'll Be Your Plaything* by Anna Szemere and András Rónai

Various Artists' *DJs do Guetto* by Richard Elliott

Czesław Niemen's *Niemen Enigmatic* by Ewa Mazierska and Mariusz Gradowski

Forthcoming Titles:

Los Rodriguez's *Sin Documentos* by Fernán del Val and Héctor Fouce

Massada's *Astaganaga* by Lutgard Mutsaers

Nuovo Canzoniere Italiano's *Bella Ciao* by Jacopo Tomatis

Amália Rodrigues's *Amália at the Olympia* by Lilla Ellen Gray

Ardit Gjebrea's *Projekt Jon* by Nicholas Tochka

Vopli Vidopliassova's *Tantsi* by Maria Sonevytsky

Édith Piaf's *Recital 1961* by David Looseley

Iannis Xenakis' *Persepolis* by Aram Yardumian

33 1/3 Oceania

Series Editors: Jon Stratton and Jon Dale

Spanning a range of artists and genres, from New Zealand noise music to Australian hip hop, **33 1/3 Oceania** offers engaging accounts of popular and culturally significant albums from the 20th and 21st centuries.

Published Titles:

John Farnham's *Whispering Jack* by Graeme Turner

Forthcoming Titles:

Regurgitator's *Unit* by Lachlan Goold and Lauren Istvandity

Ed Kuepper's *Honey Steel's Gold* by John Encarnacao

The Church's *Starfish* by Chris Gibson

Kylie Minogue's *Kylie* by Adrian Renzo and Liz Giuffre

Space Waltz's *Space Waltz* by Ian Chapman

The Dead C's *Clyma est mort* by Darren Jorgensen

John Farnham's Whispering Jack

Graeme Turner

Series Editors: Jon Stratton
and Jon Dale

BLOOMSBURY ACADEMIC
NEW YORK · LONDON · OXFORD · NEW DELHI · SYDNEY

BLOOMSBURY ACADEMIC
Bloomsbury Publishing Inc
1385 Broadway, New York, NY 10018, USA
50 Bedford Square, London, WC1B 3DP, UK
29 Earlsfort Terrace, Dublin 2, Ireland

BLOOMSBURY, BLOOMSBURY ACADEMIC and the Diana logo are
trademarks of Bloomsbury Publishing Plc

First published in the United States of America 2022

Library of Congress Cataloging-in-Publication Data

Names: Turner, Graeme, author.
Title: Whispering Jack / Graeme Turner.
Description: New York: Bloomsbury Academic, 2022. | Series: 33 1/3
Oceania | Includes bibliographical references and index. |
Summary: "An exploration of the history and cultural significance of
Australia's top-selling album by an Australian in Australia, often referred
to as Australia's unofficial national anthem"– Provided by publisher.
Identifiers: LCCN 2021047874 (print) | LCCN 2021047875 (ebook) |
ISBN 9781501382055 (hardback) | ISBN 9781501382062 (paperback) |
ISBN 9781501382079 (epub) | ISBN 9781501382086 (pdf) |
ISBN 9781501382093 (ebook other)
Subjects: LCSH: Farnham, John. Whispering Jack. | Popular music–
Australia–History and criticism.
Classification: LCC ML420.F264 W55 2022 (print) | LCC ML420.F264
(ebook) | DDC 781.640994–dc23
LC record available at https://lccn.loc.gov/2021047874
LC ebook record available at https://lccn.loc.gov/2021047875

ISBN: HB: 978-1-5013-8205-5
PB: 978-1-5013-8206-2
ePDF: 978-1-5013-8208-6
eBook: 978-1-5013-8207-9

Typeset by Deanta Global Publishing Services, Chennai, India

Series: 33 ⅓ Europe

To find out more about our authors and books visit www.bloomsbury.com
and sign up for our newsletters.

Contents

Acknowledgements

I must acknowledge a number of people who have played a significant part in initiating and completing this book. I am extremely grateful that Jon Stratton, the editor of the series and a long-time and valued colleague, thought to approach me to contribute to the newly established series, *33 1/3 Oceania*, and was enthusiastic about my choice of subject. A number of my colleagues were also pleasingly enthusiastic about the project, and understood its significance – among them are Fred D'Agostino, Toby Miller, Meaghan Morris and Anna Pertierra. Given John Farnham's unfashionability within popular music studies and the politely puzzled response my project tended to elicit from most others, their support was much appreciated. My wife, Chris, 'got it' straight away, and was extremely supportive – and perhaps relieved to find I had a manageable project to keep me occupied through the various periods of lockdown and isolation forced upon us by the pandemic. My research assistant, Dante Aloni, dug into the archives for me to unearth the press treatment of the album, and whatever academic material could be found as well; we had some enjoyable meetings in various Brisbane bars consulting on this. *Whispering Jack*'s producer, Ross Fraser, kindly made himself available for an interview, and provided me with much insight into the process and the thoughts behind the approach taken on the album. David Hirschfelder, who was behind all the keyboards and crucial to the way the arrangements on the album were imagined and orchestrated, also agreed to be interviewed, and I am extremely grateful for his generous participation. As he was the first of the production team I spoke to, I learned a great deal from our conversation, and avoided any number of naïve errors I might otherwise have made! (I hope there are none left.) Finally, I also talked with the fourth member of what was an exceptionally tight group of collaborators on the production, Doug Brady, the sound engineer, with whom again I had an informative and highly enjoyable conversation. I should also note that I approached John Farnham through his manager, Glenn Wheatley, to request an interview but that resulted in a sympathetic but firm refusal. As Glenn Wheatley informed me, Farnham hadn't done an interview for years. I had read previously that he hadn't spoken to Jane Gazzo when she was preparing her biography, so this was not a surprising response and certainly one that I respected. However, this has had the effect of forcing me to rely on his most recent biographers a little more than I would have preferred for some categories of information and background. All of that said, I take full responsibility, of course, for what follows and for the analysis it presents.

Introduction

Summer is bushfire season in Australia. Australians have become accustomed to seeing footage of bushfire outbreaks on their television screens and many have gone through the experience of personally dealing with such outbreaks directly. The summer of 2019–20, however, was something else. Australia experienced its most intense and damaging series of fires in its history. During what has become known as Black Summer, 24 million hectares of land were burnt, 3,000 homes destroyed, and 3 billion animals were killed or displaced. Thirty-four people died, including six Australian firefighters and three American aerial firefighters when their aircraft crashed. More than 65,000 people were evacuated or displaced, and 57 per cent of the population were exposed to periods of bushfire smoke. The ferocity and scale of the fires were repeatedly described as 'unprecedented' by newscasters and by emergency service spokespersons. The fires were only extinguished when torrential rains arrived in February 2020 (which then, of course, caused widespread flooding!).

The duration and persistence of the fires – they began in July 2019, but really ramped up during September before peaking in January/February 2020 – were also unprecedented, and the continuing news coverage over those months highlighted the courage and tenacity of the largely volunteer firefighters in their efforts to save life and property. National concern was deep and wide, as few were unaffected by the disaster. Consequently, a number of initiatives were established to raise funds to assist in the stricken communities' recovery, but also to acknowledge the heroism of those who had risked their lives to fight the fires. Among these initiatives, eventually raising $9 million for the cause, was the Firefight Australia Concert for National Bushfire Relief held at ANZ Stadium in Sydney on 16 February 2020.

The concert was sold out, attracting 75,000 fans; it was televised nationally live and repeated the following weekend, and featured a stellar lineup of musicians including Amy Shark, Alice Cooper and K. D. Laing (who performed 'Hallelujah'). Queen + Adam Lambert were in town and they performed a reprise of Queen's legendary 1986 Wembley Stadium Live Aid set with the crowd helping them out on 'We Will Rock You' and 'We are the Champions'. The grand finale, however, was delivered by Australia's 'national treasure' (as one report described him at the time), John Farnham, with a powerhouse rendition of his 1986 anthem 'You're the Voice'. Sharing the vocals with Olivia Newton John (another national treasure) and indigenous singer Mitch Tambo (who sang the second verse in the indigenous language, Gamilaraay), using a didgeridoo player to recast the song's opening, and sharing the stage (and a hug) with veteran Queen guitarist, Brian May, Farnham's performance was extraordinary. Adding to the spectacle, as well as the (by-now) customary pipe band coming onstage to deliver the much-loved bagpipe solo, we had a troupe of volunteer firefighters (or 'fireies' as they are called), file on stage in their high-viz vests to receive the appreciation of the crowd.

So, this was quite a moment: a powerful ritual of national unity and celebration, with a seventy-year-old semi-retired Australian rock star bringing the event to its climax by belting out a song first heard thirty-four years ago to which (seemingly) everyone in the audience knew the words and, judging from the vision on TV, just loved singing as an expression of national solidarity. There is no other Australian performer who could have generated that kind of participation from such a large and generationally diverse audience, and there are very few songs other than 'You're the Voice' to have even come close to earning the by-now customary description as Australia's 'unofficial national anthem'.[1] The story of how John Farnham, the Australian audience and 'You're the Voice' arrived at that point is an important one for the history of Australian rock and popular music, and it begins with the 1986 record album that is the subject of this book, John Farnham's *Whispering Jack*.

*   *   *

There are many reasons to devote a book in this series to *Whispering Jack*. It is still the all-time highest-selling album (heading towards 2 million sales) by an Australian artist within Australia; it hit the top of the album charts in 1986, and stayed there for twenty-six weeks; it produced four charting singles in Australia; both the album and the single of 'You're the Voice' charted in Sweden (where the single made it to No. 1), Germany (also No. 1), Ireland (No. 3), Switzerland (No. 3), the UK (No. 6), Austria (No. 6), Denmark (No. 9) as well as in the Netherlands, Norway, Belgium and Canada. It was the first album to be manufactured on CD in Australia. Its production was at the cutting edge of the music industry's adoption of new digital sampling technologies such as the Australian invention, the Fairlight CMI, which had only come up with its most advanced version the year before. And, as has been exhaustively reported in the press and in several biographies, it turned Farnham's career around. In 1985, at the point when *Whispering Jack* was in pre-production, John Farnham couldn't persuade a single record company to back him as he struggled to move past his teen-pop idol beginnings; once *Whispering Jack* was released, he commenced a journey that made him arguably the most successful solo rock and popular music artist Australia has produced.

That journey, of John Farnham as a musician and performer, is also the subject of this book. He represents a unique variant of rock stardom in Australia: the 'uncool' Everyman of rock 'n' roll, who, as the widely acknowledged 'singer's singer', could fill a stadium virtually at will. Along the way, he has acquired a personal resonance and national stature that is reflected in, among other things, his selection as Australian of the Year in 1988, Australia's Bicentennial year, and the special online exhibition celebrating his career in Australia's National Film and Sound Archive. Not a figure, one would think, that any serious account of the history of rock and popular music in Australia could ignore.

But, there's the rub. He has been ignored. Not by the mass media, who can't get enough of him, but there has been no published academic research or analysis, so far, into John Farnham's music or his career. Given his standing in the industry and in the popular imagination, this is quite an omission. In fairness, it should be acknowledged that popular music studies in Australia is a comparatively new and small discipline, and most of those who work within it have, understandably, developed a specific focus for their work. While this is an entirely legitimate strategy at the level of the individual researcher, as a general tendency it has resulted in a relatively fragmented field. So far, there is no overarching academic account or collection of works mapping the full historical field of Australian popular music, as has occurred in disciplines such as media studies or cultural studies in Australia. In fact, and this was largely the case elsewhere as well, academic studies of rock and popular music in Australia were few and far between until the 1990s. This was partly because, even internationally until the 1990s, there wasn't a widely accepted disciplinary home for the study of popular music. Admittedly, the Cambridge journal *Popular Music* was established in 1981, and there was certainly pioneering work from within sociology (Frith 1988) and musicology (Shepherd 1991), for instance, that was pushing at the boundaries of those disciplines to create room for this field of research (see Bennett et al., 1993; Shepherd and Wicke 1997 for more discussion of this issue). There was also a significant push from within music studies towards the application of more interdisciplinary methods and approaches as a way forward for the field (Middleton 1990). Along those lines, the attention directed towards rock and popular music within the development of cultural and media studies over the 1980s and 1990s, most influentially in the work of Iain Chambers (1985), Dick Hebdige (1979; 1987) and Larry Grossberg (1984; 1992), was among the factors that generated new ways of thinking about popular music (see Shuker 1993), eventually leading to the complex of established theoretical approaches outlined in later accounts of popular music studies (such as Hesmondhalgh and Negus 2002).

In Australia, there had been a presence for work on rock music within the first local cultural studies journal, the *Australian Journal of Cultural Studies*, almost from the beginning (1983), but this had largely been as a subset of work in cultural studies or, later, cultural policy studies. It wasn't until the early 1990s that an amalgam of cultural studies, sociology and musicology began to produce published outcomes that confidently situated themselves within this new field; it was also around this time that some institutional landmarks were established. Philip Hayward's contemporary music programme at Macquarie University in Sydney and his establishment of the popular music journal *Perfect Beat* in 1992, in addition to the publication of his groundbreaking edited volume *From Pop to Punk to Postmodernism: Popular music and Australian Culture from the 1960s to the 1990s* (1992a), were all highly significant interventions towards establishing the academic field in Australia. Soon, we had the first batch of PhDs in popular music studies; Shane Homan, for instance, later to become one of the leading figures in the field in Australia, completed his PhD at Macquarie University in 1999. A number of academics, including Hayward and Homan, were now able to build credible academic careers based on their research into popular music; Jon Stratton, Tony Mitchell, John Potts, Marcus Breen and Tara Brabazon were among the early adopters, with others such as Andy Bennett, Sarah Baker, Ian Rogers and Chris Gibson coming later. It has remained, however, a much smaller field in Australia than its primary enabling disciplines of cultural and media studies, although fortunately there is not much of a boundary between these fields and popular music studies. As is the case with my own work, for instance, it is not uncommon for writers in cultural studies to think in ways that refuse any strict demarcation between cultural studies and popular music studies. Importantly, there seems to be little in the way of a critical methodological difference between these two, inherently interdisciplinary, fields of research and analysis and this in turn facilitates their interaction.

As had been the case initially with cultural studies and media studies in Australia, popular music studies had to push hard for legitimacy within a conservative university system that has been at times resistant to the more interdisciplinary and non-traditional developments within the so-called new humanities. It is likely that the gradual recognition of the social and cultural significance of popular music within the academy was in part related to the fact that, over the period of the Hawke–Keating federal governments (roughly 1983–96), popular music had achieved a new level of national significance as it became one of the points of interest for the development of a more comprehensive cultural policy programme (eventuating in the Keating government's policy framework *Creative Nation* [Commonwealth of Australia 1994]). This was the case at both state and federal level, and across government portfolios ranging from the arts and cultural development to those concerned with industry and trade. Within the state arts portfolios, typically, there was interest in supporting the production of CDs, or getting bands on the road touring with state-based funding. There was also a greater interest in supporting the music produced by indigenous communities – in part driven by the international commercial success of the mixed-race band Yothu Yindi in 1992 (see Turner 1994: 132–8). Federally, the strongest support was for developing the export potential of the industry on the back of the international success of a number of Australian-based bands, but there were also major policy and regulatory debates affecting the industry's long-term future, such as that involving what was called at the time 'parallel importing' of music products and the comparatively high retail prices paid by consumers for CDs (still!) in Australia. The work of Marcus Breen (1999; 2006) remains the most fully developed and the most influential research and analysis in that space.

As some of the relevant planets come into alignment over this period, then, the expansion and development of Australian popular music studies coincided with, and was assisted by, significant shifts in cultural policy and with the increasing success Australian bands had experienced not only on the domestic market but also internationally (the standard examples of such international success include INXS, Midnight Oil, AC/DC, Men at Work and the Little River Band). Consequently, over the early 1990s, the state of the local rock music industry, perhaps surprisingly to some, took on a degree of national, political and economic significance. In addition, public interest in, and enthusiasm for, the rise of Australian music was further fuelled by a concomitant mini-boom in journalistic commentary and accounts of the history and character of Australian rock music from writers such as Glenn A. Baker, Bruce Elder, Clinton Walker, Ed Nimmervoll and Lawrie Zion.

Within most of these accounts, however, there is very little sustained attention given to the musical career and enduring popularity of Australia's most successful male solo artist, John Farnham. While, on the one hand, there are solid biographies (Gazzo 2015; Apter 2016) aimed at a popular audience which do consider him within a historicized industry; on the other hand, there are no academic articles – at all – which focus on him. I should note that he is not entirely alone here. It is also the case that other solo artists who have achieved major mainstream popular success – Delta Goodrem, Tina Arena, even Kylie Minogue – have been largely ignored as well. The attention of the field has been elsewhere. *Perfect Beat*, for instance, has pursued its strong interest in music from the Pacific region, while each of the leading researchers has developed their own specializations. Tony Mitchell, for instance, has been primarily concerned with investigating Australian versions of rap; Jon Stratton (2007) and Tara Brabazon (2005) both focused on the rich and distinctive post-punk music scene in Perth; and there is a strong body of work that looks at various aspects of the industry's structure rather than at the careers of individual performers – Shane Homan (2003), for instance, has done that. There have been more general accounts, but they have been limited in their scope and scale. David Nicoll's *Dig* (2017) provides a historian's exhaustively detailed overview of the industry from 1960 to 1985, but it is really only the first half of Stratton's *Australian Rock* that attempts an academic analysis of the local industry since then – and that was published in 2007. Most recently, Stratton, Dale and Mitchell's 'anthology' of Australian albums (2020) responds to this issue in a distinctive way by collecting a series of essays on key albums, with a concentration on music 'from the 21st century', but the gap in the academic field remains. Similarly, the gaze of the rock journalists has been largely fixed on the pub-rock culture of the 1980s and its successors, or upon the various configurations of the alternative-indie scene that first appeared in the late 1970s and gradually merged with the mainstream over the 1990s and beyond (Engleheart 2010; Walker 2005; Zion 1988; Walker, Hogan, and Beilharz 2012; Neal 2021).

While there is no criticism intended here of individual researchers freely choosing their areas of interest, I think it is also fair to suggest that there may well be a set of informal and perhaps unexamined preferences in play which influence what kind of music turns out to be the subject of a popular music studies in Australia. Some of this averted gaze may reflect a dismissive response to Farnham's early career as a teen idol pop star: his first No. 1 was the novelty hit 'Sadie (The Cleaning Lady)', released in 1967, and he continued to churn out (mostly) lightweight pop hits over the next seven years. This seriously undermined his attempts to achieve credibility as an adult rock performer at the point in his career which this book examines. That said, even in John Farnham's later career when he had fully established himself as a major force in the Australian music industry, and despite a three-year stint (1982–5) fronting an established arena-rock band, the Little River Band (LRB), in the United States and Europe, he remained something of an anomaly in the industry – a major rock star who just doesn't seem all that rock 'n' roll. Indeed, as a performer, and as a personality, John Farnham is still described, oxymoronically perhaps, as the 'nice guy of rock 'n' roll'.

In the oppositional culture of attitude and excess that is fundamental to rock music mythology, as well as to the rock journalism which reports on the industry, being the nice guy is not necessarily a good thing – and nor is it, it seems, a good fit for popular music studies. On the one hand, as a performer, Farnham lacks the aggression or grittiness of those fronting the bands that had emerged from the heart of Australian rock 'n' roll, the pub-rock circuit, over the 1970s and 1980s. As I have remarked elsewhere, John Farnham's onstage persona is a million miles from AC/DC's Bon Scott, or INXS's Michael Hutchence, or even Jimmy Barnes (Turner 1989: 2). On the other hand, neither does he occupy the alternative/indie, romantic, artist-outsider persona of someone like Steve Kilbey of The Church or David McComb of the Triffids. Rather, and similar perhaps to Kylie Minogue, Farnham is a much-loved and extremely talented performer who managed to succeed in the rock industry despite the apparent 'ordinariness', the lack of edginess, carried by their professional personae. Perhaps as a consequence of this, whenever rock journalists or popular music studies researchers try to map the major streams that flow into Australian rock and popular music – and there is a considerable variety of such attempts – there is never a location found for John Farnham. Within such accounts of the contexts, taste patterns or subcultural formations used to identify the most significant components of the Australian music scene – pub-rock, alternative/indie rock or post-punk, for instance – Farnham is either left out entirely or cited only as an 'exception to the rule' (Walker, Hogan, and Beilharz 2012: 125). It is likely, then, that the difficulty in accommodating Farnham's career within the established critical and analytical orthodoxies around the key formations in Australian rock 'n' roll histories, notwithstanding the scale and longevity of his mainstream success, may be the key reason why there is so little academic discussion of his work within studies of Australian popular music.

This is the challenge that this book addresses, as it sets out to fill a major gap in the academic literature on Australian popular music. John Farnham is the most successful Australian rock singer of all time, and he has managed to maintain that position more or less from the moment in November 1986 when *Whispering Jack* started its run at the top of the charts, and as the string of charting singles was launched with 'You're the Voice' that same year. It is time we properly considered this musician and the album that produced a stack of arena-ready power ballads and rock anthems that are still being sung by packed audiences in the largest venues available in Australia today. This book is a step towards filling a notable lacuna in the Australian field of popular music studies, by examining *Whispering Jack* in the way it has long deserved: as an important album not just because it revived John Farnham's career, but because of its significant contribution to the history of Australian popular music.

Let me conclude this introduction by providing a brief outline of what follows. Chapter 1, inevitably, engages in some retelling of the backstory of Farnham's transition from 'Johnny to John', and from an industry untouchable to a dazzling success. This story, however, has been told often and well elsewhere (Zuel 2000; Nimmervoll 2004; Gazzo 2015; Adams 2015; Apter 2016a), and so the distinctive contribution this chapter will make is to situate the album within certain shifts in Australian media and popular culture over the 1980s and within the music industry itself. The broader context for the success of *Whispering Jack* includes quite a number of enabling factors: the rise of FM radio and the consequent death of 'teen radio'; demographic shifts in the audience for mainstream rock and popular music; the winding down of the 1980s enthusiasm for the so-called Australian sound and the implicit embrace of a more international model for Australian-recorded music production; the associated development and take-up of digital technologies for performing and recording, and the heightened presence for keyboards generally and the synthesizer in particular that, for instance, accompanied the wave of synth-pop coming out of, largely, the UK and Europe. More challenging than enabling, however, was the continuing power of the prevailing patterns of rock music's street-cred that placed a significant obstacle in the path of Farnham's mission to reinvent himself.

Chapter 2 is focused on *Whispering Jack* itself, not only by discussing each of the individual tracks and Farnham's performance as a singer but also by examining the particular approach taken to the production. Responding to the shifts which were to make the synthesizer the 'signature sound of the 1980s' (Marks 2015), and setting out to produce something that was at the cutting edge of the current trends in contemporary rock music, the album is the product of the collaborative creative partnership between Farnham, producer Ross Fraser, keyboards star David Hirschfelder and sound engineer Doug Brady. Dispensing with live drums and (except for two tracks) live bass, the album is distinguished by, among many other things, its extensive use of keyboards, samplers and sequencers. Finally, the chapter deals with the album's reception, the longevity of its career and how it affected John Farnham's standing and credibility in the music industry in Australia.

The first single from *Whispering Jack*, 'You're the Voice', has become something of a popular music and cultural phenomenon in its own right. Covered a number of times by other singers, it is only Farnham's version that has reached stellar levels of visibility and recognition. The song has developed a career independent of the album. It is the subject of a separate exhibition in Australia's National Film and Sound Archive, and, as noted at the beginning of this Introduction, it has become a regular feature of events of national celebration and national appeals[2] and continues to elicit vigorous participation from crowds wherever it is performed. Chapter 3 is devoted to examining the career of this iconic song and its ascent to the status of Australia's unofficial national anthem.

In the final chapter, some of the consequences of *Whispering Jack*'s success are discussed. The album is probably the centrepiece for the period in Australian popular music that has been labelled as baby-boomer rock, but it also introduced Australia to the kind of solo artist arena events that had been relatively common for some of the guitar bands and international headliners but had not, until this point, been common for Australian-based solo acts – no matter how big they had become. Australian music, and indeed popular music generally, had always had its roots in suburbia, but in many ways this album took rock music into a more broadly based mainstream than had existed for any other artist. To some extent, that broad base has become a recognizable market now, extending the reach of other artists such as Jimmy Barnes. It is also interesting to note that some of Farnham's most significant hits – on this album and on subsequent albums such as *Age of Reason* – were about social issues, or political rights, rather than the perennial love songs of mainstream pop. Finally, there is the question of John Farnham's iconic personal status within Australian national culture; this is discussed through an analysis of his so-called ordinariness, and his unique connection to an exceptionally broad-based and loyal national audience.

1 The backstory
From Johnny to John

In the beginning, it was Johnny Farnham, the teen pop star, who was crowned *TV Week*'s 'King of Pop' five years in a row during the late 1960s and early 1970s. 'Sadie (The Cleaning Lady)' was No. 1 in the singles charts for five weeks in 1968, and became the biggest-selling Australian single of the decade; it made Johnny Farnham a household name. However, the comprehensiveness with which he was identified with a song that was more George Formby than Elvis Presley meant that he experienced great difficulty moving from an ephemeral teen stardom into a more long-term and credible career as an adult rock performer. A video included in Australia's National Film and Sound Archive online exhibition celebrating Farnham's career, taken from the *TV Week* and Channel 10 'King of Pop' awards of 1971, reveals how far that world of teen stardom was from where he might have wanted to be as an adult performer a decade later. The award was presented to him by Liberace (!), and involved accepting (and wearing) a large and silly fake fur-trimmed crown (Liberace, when he sees it, says 'I want it, I want it!'). While doing his best to cooperate, Farnham looks extremely uncomfortable.

At this time he was managed by Darrell Sambell, whose strategy for helping Farnham to leave that world behind was to aim for that most familiar (and usually elusive) destination for pop music stars at the time: the role of the 'all round entertainer'. Accordingly, Johnny Farnham appeared in television sitcoms and soaps, hosted 'white floor' TV variety series, sang cabaret and headlined stage musicals to build his all-round profile. But he still could not escape the consequences of his teen-pop star history. By the late 1970s, he was reduced to playing what Bernard Zuel (2016) has called 'the rubber chicken circuit': the local services and RSL (Returned Services League) clubs whose revenue was built on poker machines but who also provided variety entertainment (from cabaret acts, to magic shows, to popular music bands) to their members. (The 'rubber chicken' referred to the quality of the food served in these venues). There are plenty of accounts of just how dispiriting that experience could be for many of the pop and rock musicians who found themselves playing to small and often disinterested audiences rather than to a roomful of fans (see, for instance, Apter 2016a: 87–8). Farnham's eventual route out of that circuit involved a change in management. He parted company with Darrel Sambell and signed with someone who supported his vision of a future as a rock singer, the Little River Band's manager, Glenn Wheatley. Farnham changed his name to the more adult 'John', and began the task of earning credibility and respect as a serious contemporary rock performer.

In that endeavour, he became something of a regular on one of the few television outlets for local rock and pop musicians at the time, the Nine Network's *Hey Hey It's Saturday*. Eventually running for twenty-eight years, from 1971 to 1999, *Hey Hey It's Saturday* had started out as a children's variety and game show on Saturday mornings but had attracted such a loyal late teens and young adult audience – appreciating its amiable anarchy and slyly inserted adult jokes as they recovered from the big Friday night out – that it was moved into a 6.30 pm slot on Saturday evenings where the baby boomers could pick it up before heading out for the night. *Hey Hey* responded to that audience by promoting Australian bands and performers. Giving the music industry valuable mass exposure on a Saturday night, it addressed an audience for local musicians that was much broader than the audience for the pub-rock that was dominant for so much of that time. Farnham's performances on *Hey Hey* most probably played a part in laying the basis for the breadth of his popular appeal later on. He was also a regular on the various late-night television chat and variety shows hosted by American entertainer Don Lane over the 1970s and 1980s; this audience usually skewed old, but Lane was a devoted fan and promoted Farnham tirelessly. Nevertheless, and valuable though it was, one would imagine that this kind of exposure was still a long way from where Farnham would have hoped to be.

The first point at which most Australians might have registered John Farnham's reinvention of himself as a singer was probably through his contribution to a Royal Command concert in 1980, when he performed his re-interpretation of the Beatles' song 'Help'. Broadcast live on national television, this was an original and arresting re-casting of that song, and it eventually became Farnham's first charting single in seven years (it reached No. 8). The album on which it appeared, *Uncovered*, was a hit when it was released in 1980: it formally launched his change of name, it ticked the box of being 'a little more rock 'n' roll' (as Farnham described it in a TV interview[1]), and its success enabled him to take a band on the road to tour around Australia. Apart from 'Help', however, the material wasn't especially distinctive (most of the remaining songs were written by Little River Band's Graham Goble) and in subsequent interviews Farnham has implied that it didn't really reflect the kinds of work he most wanted to record (he says that he may have been 'led by the nose' on song selection ([Gazzo 2015: 177]). While a good start, but still only making it to No. 20 on the album charts, *Uncovered* wasn't quite the rebooting that his career needed.

It is understandable, if in retrospect possibly unfortunate, that he would take the next big opportunity offered to him – to replace Glenn Shorrock as the lead singer for the Little River Band (LRB). For some observers at the time, it seemed like a bit of a stretch for Farnham to front a rock band, even one as comparatively mellow as LRB, and it did take him out of Australia for an extended period. While there is no doubt he delivered in his stint as LRB's frontman over 1982–5, this period also coincided with a more critical reception of LRB's records, a marked decline in their commercial viability, and the gradual withdrawal of their record label's support (Gazzo, among others, suggests that the American executives at Capitol did not approve of the switch from Shorrock to Farnham [2015: 183]). It was not an easy period for LRB or for their lead singer. There were ructions in the band, disputes about the selection of material and even concerns raised about how Farnham should present himself on stage (he was asked to tone down his characteristically exuberant stage persona). Apter (2016a) and Gazzo (2015) both report that Farnham learnt a lot from what seems like a personally and financially bruising experience, and consequently vowed to take on more direct personal control after he returned to Australia and began to resurrect his solo career. Unfortunately, though, by the mid-1980s in Australia, he had become almost untouchable for the industry: no recent hits, no recording contract, no prospects, and he was broke. At this time, 'Farnham's name', says Apter (2016b), 'was music industry poison. No record label would touch him. He hadn't had a number one hit since 1969's "Raindrops Keep Falling on My Head", and was still known to many as Johnny Farnham, the pretty popstar'.

Looking back now it is hard to understand why John Farnham was not afforded greater respect as a singer at the time. Apter quotes Farnham as observing ruefully that, at this point in time, 'people never saw me as being a credible singer' (Apter 2016a: 141). Sam See, the former member of Sherbet who played in the Little River Band alongside Farnham, and who was also a member of Farnham's touring band for a time, confirms that judgement, noting that audiences were mixed in their reactions to him: 'We'd do a lot of gigs where the blokes would sort of regard him as a lightweight and I don't think that changed until after *Whispering Jack*.' (Gazzo 2015: 177). My own personal experience as a working musician in the early 1980s complicates that account slightly; I recollect very clearly that he was talked about by other musicians as the 'singer's singer' back then, and their criticism focused on his choice of material rather than on his talent or ability. Apter (2016b) points to that as well, as an issue that was explicitly addressed by the team involved in developing *Whispering Jack* – producer Ross Fraser, keyboardist David Hirschfelder and Farnham himself: 'Farnham needed to prove he could handle weightier emotional material – he made inroads with [the] 1980s rendering of the Beatles *Help* – but he also needed to update his sound. Technology was rapidly changing; he wanted to make a contemporary-sounding record.' The challenge for *Whispering Jack*, then, was considerable: find a new set of career-defining songs, produce a technically cutting-edge album and get someone to release it!

The Australian music industry in the 1980s

Understanding that challenge involves some consideration of the context in which it was located – the industrial and cultural formations that shaped the Australian rock and popular music industry in the 1980s. John Farnham had a very particular relation to that context. As Jane Gazzo points out, Farnham's history as a rock musician is not like most stories about starting out in the industry. He hadn't had to 'live in a grubby share house, starving or struggling to pay rent, or busking on the streets to earn money. He'd quit his job [as a plumber] two days before his debut single came out and had never looked back' (2015: 182–3). Most crucially, unlike contemporaries such as the members of INXS, AC/DC, the Angels or Australian Crawl, for instance, he hadn't worked his way up through the pub-rock circuit, and for quite a while that actually mattered. Over the 1970s, the pub circuit had become the standard training ground for the industry; it was seen almost as a kind of apprenticeship, which every aspiring rock musician needed to undertake in order to achieve their licence to rock 'n' roll. Consequently, within the calculus of 'cool' that has always calibrated reputations in the rock music industry, and notwithstanding the fact that he had certainly paid his dues working in a range of equally challenging platforms and venues, Farnham had a significant deficit to overcome. Maybe that is why the stint with LRB seemed like a good idea at the time; it might have lent him some rock 'n' roll credibility. Unfortunately, as Sam See's comment quoted earlier suggests, it seems like it didn't much help. Without having worked his way up through the pub-rock circuit, the five-time King of Pop faced a long struggle for respect within the world of 1980s Australian rock 'n' roll.

Within the popular memory of Australian music over the 1970s and 1980s, pub-rock has been extensively mythologized around a particular breed of hard rock, guitar-based bands such as the Aztecs, Rose Tattoo and the Angels (Engleheart 2010). Notwithstanding this mythology, it is probably important to point out that the pub circuit wasn't just populated by bands like them. It also included, for instance, soft-rock singer–songwriters such as Richard Clapton or Brian Cadd, soul divas such as Renee Geyer, folk-rock bands such as Goanna, country rockers such as the Dingoes and the various punk and post-punk elements of the alternative, 'inner city sound' documented by Clinton Walker (1982, 2005). Like most myths, however, it does have some genuine substance behind it: the undeniable industrial centrality of the 'masculine and beer-soaked pub circuits', which 'produced [a] blunt and uncompromising pub culture' (Homan 2006: 243), as well as successive generations of Australian rock bands. The size and character of the pub venues varied quite a lot (Oldham

2013): in inner Sydney or Melbourne, for instance, they could be quite intimate neighbourhood pubs presenting niche or emerging bands, but in the outer suburbs of Sydney or Melbourne or Perth they were often enormous characterless barns designed solely to absorb the large crowds attracted by the more established bands (Turner 1992). Some venues would programme music most nights across the whole week, often setting up longstanding 'residencies' on set nights, while others would concentrate on the weekend with the Saturday or Sunday afternoon 'session' a particular drawcard. These were Dionysian events; what people wanted to do at the pub was to 'rage'.[2] Culturally, as the coinage of that term would suggest, pub-rock was situated right smack in the middle of rock music's mythology of excess, indulgence, rebellion and 'attitude'. As Walker, Hogan and Beilhartz (2012: 121) describe it, pub-rock was 'muscular, loud, white and proudly bogan.[3] It was working class and slyly subversive: as it sang of sex, drugs and rock 'n' roll, it also announced itself as the hegemonic culture of suburbia's disaffected youth.' Along the same lines, in our *Myths of Oz: Reading Australian Popular Culture* (Fiske, Hodge and Turner 1987: 17–25), in a section dealing with youth, rock 'n' roll and the Australian pub, my co-authors and I talked about pub-rock venues stripping the rock performance back to its most basic and affordable elements, effectively 'proletarianising' the rock concert for suburban consumption. Interestingly, while notionally national in scale, in many cases the pub circuit also worked to localize audiences around their own bands, creating an element of tribalism that linked the fans, the bands, the suburb and the particular pubs identified as supporting them. These were the venues, then, which produced the punk rock of the Saints in the 1970s, as well as the post-punk and alternative bands that were so successful in the 1980s, such as INXS, Midnight Oil or The Triffids (Walker 2005). But, as we've seen, they didn't produce John Farnham. While he has always come across as an authentic and unpretentious character on stage, it was not the sweaty, aggressive, masculinist persona of the pub rockers. Farnham was cheeky but likeable, suburban rather than urban, the everyman rather than the superstar, the nice guy rather than the guy with attitude.

There was another system of distinction that is relevant here. Homan (2006b: 4) has talked about the implications embedded in the industry's hierarchical differentiation between the original performer and the cover artist, or between the artist and the entertainer: 'while original composers saw themselves as artists *and* entertainers, the same group placed cover musicians distinctly (and disdainfully) in the "entertainers' box"', he says. Such a distinction is also inferred when McIntyre (2007: 85) discusses what he describes as the Romantic conception of the rock musician during the period under consideration: that 'preferred rock artists to pop or soul performers, albums over singles, self-contained bands or solo artists . . . writing their own songs, rather than singers who worked with arrangers, session musicians and songwriters in putting together a package'. An Australian version of this in the 1970s and 1980s might be said to have preferred rock bands over pop stars, originals over covers, independents over corporate labels, 'alternative' over 'commercial', and those who had paid their dues in the pubs rather than, say, those who had built a career through television or variety shows (the reality TV show, *Popstars*, when it turned up in the early 2000s, attracted precisely this kind of criticism and was largely dismissed by the music industry).

However, things were changing by the time we head into the mid-1980s. The connection between the so-called Australian sound (Zion 1988), the pub-rock circuit and the strategic investment preferences of the commercial industry was starting to fragment. According to Homan, to some extent this acknowledged what had largely been the case already: 'despite theories of a distinct "Australian sound" that was grounded in pub-rock, and visions of an isolated industry producing original musics, the local pattern has been to only exploit those artists deemed to possess an international aesthetic' (2006: 244.) And while there was considerable debate within Australian popular music studies over this period about the existence of an identifiable 'Australian sound' (Homan 2006: 244; Hayward 1992b: 3–6), both Homan and I were probably among the majority[4] in arguing that, at best and given the already thoroughly transnational character of the popular music industry, any 'Australian sound' could only ever be 'an inflection', or 'the distinctive modification of an already internationally established musical style' (Turner 1992: 13). That said, there was a short period when some music consumers overseas took a different view. There was what Glen A Baker (1986b) describes as the 'Australian craze' – American interest in signing Australian performers as 'novelty acts' on the back of the success of Men at Work's 1981 album *Business as Usual*, and their single, 'The Land Down Under' (the single was No. 1 in the American charts for fifteen weeks!). However, once that died down, argues Baker, local labels and management were focused on producing material that was 'internationally acceptable' – in terms of production standards first, but also in terms of their genre placement and their perceived 'contemporariness' (and exactly how this was defined in practice was, of course, crucial). Locally based labels increased their investment in local acts with international potential, with some labels who had never invested much locally before, such as Polygram, joining that trend (at that time, only one of the six major record companies in Australia, Festival, was Australian owned). What Baker characterizes as the 'placeless internationalism' of bands, such as AC/DC and INXS, constituted what now looks like a definitive move away from the mythologized Aussie pub-rock culture.

When commentators on the period investigate the ways in which the Australian music industry changed over the early 1980s, they highlight a number of factors which both drove and emerged from the shifting industry dynamics of the time. For example, the key features of the post-punk rock music industry in Australia from the late 1970s onwards that are laid out in Walker, Hogan and Beilhartz's (2012) history include the following: the rise in the importance of albums over singles from the mid-1960s onwards (over the 1970s, sales of albums outnumbered singles three to one); the shift from local and independent labels towards what they call corporate (that is, international and foreign-owned) rock which was more or less complete by the end of the 1990s (Festival closed down in 2005); and the gradual ascent to both local and international viability for an increasing number of Australian-based bands. There was also the accelerating sophistication of production technology as multitrack and digital methods were emerging, and a major shift in the relative power of radio and television in building an audience for popular music. In relation to this last factor, although the long-running weekly ABC TV music programme *Countdown* finished in 1987, *MTV* had already arrived by then and with it came the power of the music video. Around the world, radio was losing its longstanding capacity to break new acts as much of its power had been transferred effectively to music video – which, in the early days of MTV, had acquired the status of an art form in its own right rather than serving merely as the promotional vehicle for another product (hence, The Buggles' 1979 hit single, 'Video Killed the Radio Star').

Finally, Walker, Hogan and Beilhartz argue that the diversification of genres, of labels and of audiences eventually meant that pub-rock 'ran out of steam' as a commercially dominant genre. In the competition with electronic dance music, hip hop, world music and acoustic/roots music, they suggest, 'rock music lost its primacy' (124). I wouldn't go quite that far; I would regard the situation they describe as having more to do with the way that rock music was itself mutating – in particular at this point in time, in its response to the challenge to the centrality of the guitar posed by the increasing use of keyboards and synthesizers in, for instance, the various iterations of new wave 'synth-pop' in the early 1980s. However, when one assesses this situation, few would deny that the trend towards internationalization noted earlier was implicated in the significant shift away from guitar-based bands, and towards the more diverse sounds and genres of adult contemporary rock.

In his biography of John Farnham, *Playing to Win*, Jeff Apter talks about the influence of this global tendency. 'The mid-80s,' he says, 'were ruled by the polished sounds of such local acts as Real Life ... and Mondo Rock and INXS, while internationals like A-Ha, the Eurythmics, Madonna and Foreigner were everywhere'. The common element across such acts, Apter suggests, was 'their studio slickness; in order to get played on the radio, and thereby compete on the charts, a record needed to sound huge'. He cites Bruce Springsteen's 'Born in the USA' as an example of the type of 'rolling sonic thunder' that Farnham needed to capture in *Whispering Jack* if he was to 'compete' (2016a: 141). A further common element that Apter does not mention specifically, but which is implicit in his citing Real Life, A-ha, and the Eurythmics, is the central role of keyboards in creating this 'huge' sound over the 1980s. In addition to the traditional keyboard instruments, the developing capabilities and widespread use of the synthesizer, along with the sampler, drum machines and the sequencer, were changing the composition, the production, the performance and the sounds of rock and popular music. Even the once-standard configuration of the rock band was under revision; keyboards-based UK pop bands such as Depeche Mode and Orchestral Manoeuvres in the Dark, for instance, were performing without a drummer. Established artists such as Stevie Wonder and Peter Gabriel were experimenting with the Fairlight CMI, looking to electronics to create the 'huge' production effect that Apter describes. While the synth-pop influence was not as strong in Australia as it was in the UK – significantly, electronic dance music was not as important here at that stage – the 'rudimentary equipment' assembled to begin pre-production on *Whispering Jack* (a drum machine, a Yamaha keyboard, a sequencer and a Fairlight CMI) were 'very much instruments of the moment' (Apter 2016a: 143–4) nonetheless. The embrace of the keyboard-dominated sound of the 1980s was a significant shift in the dynamics shaping mainstream post-punk rock and popular music in Australia.

The changes in radio

What I have been describing above were relatively gradual modulations or progressions in tastes and choices, but there was greater volatility in the broadcasting industry. Radio experienced major disruptions which resulted in changes that dramatically affected the broadcasting formats that were commercially viable, the audience demographics addressed within this commercial environment and the kinds of music that got played. While the competition from music video mentioned earlier would certainly present a significant challenge as the 1980s progressed, it was the introduction of FM radio to Australia that proved to be the first crucial disruptor for broadcasters of popular music. Held off by regulatory delays for many years, and always resisted by the major players in the industry due to fears that it would pose a commercial threat to the dominant Top 40 radio stations on the AM band, FM radio arrived in Australia in 1980. As the existing AM proprietors had predicted, it was immediately successful, expanding the radio audience and seizing up to 50 per cent of that audience in each capital city. This rapid early success was due to FM's capacity to broadcast in stereo, and to deliver a higher-quality sound than AM could achieve at the time. Since that competitive advantage was most evident in the music they played, it was inevitable that most commercial FM programming formats would focus almost solely on music. To attract their audience early, the new commercial FM stations started out playing back-to-back tracks with minimal interruptions from advertising. Typically, AM commercial broadcasting was riddled with ads, and so FM promoted special ad-free sessions of uninterrupted music, lasting anything up to an hour initially. Initially, too, they had extensive playlists, which were not just drawn from the Top 40, and adopted low rates of rotation. These strategies wound down, however, as they learnt more about their market and as their AM competitors withdrew from the contest. (Some AM stations converted to FM, and in 1985, AM stereo was introduced but it still couldn't match the sound quality of FM stereo.)

The second major disruption within the radio industry was in part driven by the changes in ownership and control that had occurred right across the electronic media in Australia during the 1980s – in almost all cases resulting in higher concentrations of ownership and an increasing push towards a greater degree of national networking for television and radio. FM radio in Australia consolidated around two (more or less national) networks – Hoyts and Austereo. Notably, Farnham's manager, Glenn Wheatley, was one of the major players here. Through his company, Hoyts Media, Wheatley took over virtually all the top-rating FM stations on the east coast over the period 1986–7, to the point where Glenn A. Baker estimated that, by 1988, Wheatley's radio stations reached 11 million Australians (in a population at the time of 16 million), and 70 per cent of the Australian audience under thirty listened to one of his stations (Baker 1988: 58.). (He had also, according to Baker, 'taken over virtually the entire A&R operations' of the major record label BMG/RCA Australia, while still managing Farnham, Glenn Shorrock and the pop band Pseudo Echo' [61]). The concentration of ownership and the increasing degree of networking that ensued (the mixed success of radio networking across capital city markets is another story!) were among the factors which influenced the consolidation of a relatively standard programming format across the industry around an AOR (album-oriented) mix of 'classic tracks' or 'rock memories' together with a narrow selection of new additions to the weekly playlist. Formats were no longer structured around high-charting singles releases; the previously dominant AM Top 40 or 'teen' radio format more or less disappeared (Turner 1993), although the sales charts themselves retained their key place within the industry's economy. Prior to all of this, Top 40 pop music had been a highly profitable area for AM radio, with (for instance) Sydney's market leader 2SM achieving a 24 per cent audience share in 1979 (Homan 2014: 284). But AM lost the battle for music audiences once FM established itself and gradually shifted its standard programming formats towards talk as a result.

By the early 1990s, the dominant formats for contemporary music radio had been more or less settled – quite similar to the music formats still current, in fact, although talk, particularly at breakfast and 'drive', has made a major comeback on the FM band. Ed Jonker (1992) describes the dominant formats of contemporary music radio at that time as contemporary rock aimed mainly at eighteen- to twenty-four-year-olds, but he notes that the playlists were relatively conservative in terms of how they were curated. While the independent recording sector was large in terms of the numbers of artists and labels, 'playlists were still dominated by the majors' (1992: 25). This made it hard for local independents to get airplay, even though a national cultural policy setting mandated a minimum quota of local content had to be met by commercial broadcasters: the minimum percentage of Australian-produced music to be played was 20 per cent in the 1980s, and rose to 25 per cent for adult contemporary commercial stations in 1992. While this did provide assistance to the industry, the quota didn't differentiate between new and old material and so there was little incentive for stations to prioritize the programming of new music from local musicians. Consequently, new music struggled to be heard while the makeup of the playlists was influenced by the presumed preferences of the audience for classic 'hits and memories' or what John Potts (1992) labelled 'heritage rock'. Although the ABC's youth music station, Triple J, which started in Sydney in 1981 before going national in 1989, offered an alternative here by vigorously championing new local music, the music played on commercial FM radio did tend to support Jonker's criticism that formats tended to follow 'well-established patterns [with music that] . . . is performed by well-known artists or their heirs apparent' (1992: 25).

As mentioned earlier, a key means through which the FM music playlist sought to differentiate itself from its predecessors in AM Top 40 formats was to shift away from a dependence upon record sales as a way of selecting tracks to add to the playlist. This became an article of faith in the emerging industry as programmers were determined to manage their music choices through their own judgement about the 'consistency of "fit" within individual station identities' (Homan 2007: 98). Homan notes that such a concern continued a long 'tradition of [Australian radio] stations denouncing the "bad" music offered by their rivals'. However, the fetishization of the station identities as the key factor in reaching their audience did take that tradition to a new level. In the 1980s and 1990s, for instance, the Triple M network refused to play Kylie Minogue on the basis of 'her "pop" credential that did not require a pub rock apprenticeship' (Homan 2007: 98). Perverse as it might seem now given how thoroughly she has outgrown that teen audience, not only could Kylie Minogue be at No. 2 in the Australian singles charts in 1988 and not get FM radio airplay (Turner 1993) but she also experienced that restriction for at least the next decade. The key methodology that was employed to tailor the FM playlist to the station identity was a massive investment in audience research. As I have outlined at length elsewhere, the widespread take-up of 'callout research' – market research by telephone which played short clips of tracks to the person on the other end of the phone and sought their reaction – was operated in such a way as to effectively privilege recognition. Rather than previewing reactions to a range of new tracks to assess their *likely* level of fit with the station's identity, they were primarily an enquiry into 'what is *already* being played, into what is *already* recognizable, into what the audience *already* likes about the radio station' (Turner 1993: 149, emphasis in the original). This constituted a further barrier for new material seeking to be added to the playlist, and represented, over time, a dramatic reframing of the commercial strategies for music radio programming in Australia.

There are additional factors we might mention, but these are the key ones in play. For our purposes here, what is worth noting, and this notwithstanding the conservatism of the standard FM playlist, is that by the time Farnham returned home and commenced the process of producing *Whispering Jack*, some of the key conditions framing the industry had become a little more hospitable for his proposed career trajectory. Although he was still stuck with his non-rock backstory, the market for the kind of music he wanted to create had become more receptive. As I noted earlier, while there was no diminution in the national interest in producing Australian music, mainstream rock in Australia was not only finding that it could compete with international performers more successfully, but it was also more strongly influenced by the diversity of international trends and by the production standards of the leading international performers. In terms of its production standards and in its close engagement with the sounds of contemporary music, *Whispering Jack* was at the leading edge of what was being done internationally. Interestingly, too, the context for the consumption of rock music was on its way towards significant change as well. The adult contemporary brand of mainstream rock, fuelled and propagated through FM radio and music video, was breaking out of its tribal subcultures and urban scenes into something that was more happily suburban, everyday and less 'scene-driven' than before. Increasingly cross-generational, mainstream AOR contemporary rock developed a broad-based appeal among many adults as well as adolescents (Jonker, 1992; 25), thus laying the ground for the scale of the popular success the album – and Farnham himself – was about to enjoy.

The task ahead

It may not have seemed that way to Farnham, his producer Ross Fraser and keyboards musician David Hirschfelder when they set to work on the album in the winter of 1985. The conditions for Farnham, personally, at the time were not good. As Farnham recalls it:

> I was in significant debt at the time. I'd made some very bad business decisions and I was really in a bit of trouble. I had to sell my house and my car. We were renting this place, I hated it, it was just not me but it had a basement. So we set up in the basement and did all the pre-production on *Whispering Jack* for 18 hours a day. (Adams 2018)

Finally, the singer was involved in precisely what Jane Gazzo suggested he had bypassed at the beginning of his career – a classic rock muso's struggle for survival that would only be successful if his music attracted an audience.

There was much to worry about on that count because, at that point, the production had not attracted a label to cover its costs. In the end, Wheatley mortgaged his house to finance the album's production and, as has been widely reported, when the album finally was produced, Wheatley had to release it on his own label before RCA eventually took it on. He sent it around the radio stations in a plain wrapper in an attempt to hide the fact that it was by John Farnham, although that apparently didn't fool anybody. Press accounts include numerous stories of FM radio programmers (for instance, from Triple M) telling Wheatley that they would never play anything by Farnham, because of 'Sadie'. That certainly fits with the kind of programming strategies laid out earlier. Finally, however, Farnham's live performances promoting the album on television – the one most commonly cited was on *Hey Hey Its Saturday* – generated so many listener requests for 'You're the Voice' that eventually FM radio had little alternative but to play it. Farnham may not have been 'a fashion leader' nor 'a heartthrob', as Rick Blaskey, head of European marketing for RCA had said when considering the European release, but 'the music [said] it all' (Billboard 1987).

And that's what we will talk about next.

2 *Whispering Jack –* the album

Before commencing this discussion of the album, I must acknowledge that this chapter draws significantly upon personal interviews with *Whispering Jack*'s producer Ross Fraser, keyboards whiz and musical director David Hirschfelder and sound engineer Doug Brady. I will be quoting directly from these conversations from time to time, but I need to acknowledge that what I learnt from these conversations goes well beyond the direct quotes that appear. This chapter could not have been written without their contributions, and I am very grateful for their generosity in giving me their time.

Good songs, good beats and the energy of rock

Both David Hirschfelder and Ross Brady talked to me about the experience of workshopping *Whispering Jack* in John Farnham's garage over a period of some months in 1985, working through boxes of demo cassettes to find the right songs, experimenting with the sounds they could coax out of Hirschfelder's phalanx of keyboards and Fraser's drum machines, and at times just 'mucking about' with the technology to see what they could come up with. There were some very clear guiding principles directing this project, however. As Hirschfelder explains it, they wanted to produce an album that had 'strong melodic songs, with good lyrics, good beats that would get people moving in their seat or on the dance floor', and an album that had 'the energy of rock' but the sophistication in the production of something 'quite orchestrated, almost like we were orchestrating without an orchestra'.

It may have proven difficult to find the right 'strong melodic songs' for the album (at one point, Hirschfelder says, they were getting worried because they had only found eight songs and they needed ten), but, of those upon which they settled, four turned out to be good enough to wind up as charting singles ('You're the Voice', 'Pressure Down', 'Reasons' and 'A Touch of Paradise'). In addition, there are at least three more that, for my ears, could also have been in contention for release as a single ('No-One Comes Close', 'Going, Going, Gone' and 'Love To Shine'). All of these songs either contained seductive hooks, or they built towards rising, and in a couple of cases anthemic, arena-rock choruses. The eventual song selection, according to music journalist Glen A. Baker, was 'fiercely Australian oriented', with songwriting contributions from Mondo Rock's Eric McCosker and Ross Wilson, Gulliver Smith (ex-Company Caine), Sam See (ex-Sherbet and LRB) and the Jon Kennet–Dave Skinner team (1986: 77). Other contributors included Harry Bogdanov and Kiki Dee from the UK as well as the four UK-based writers of 'You're the Voice' (Chris Thompson, Keith Reid, Maggie Ryder and Andy Quinta). One song ('Going, Going, Gone') was written by John Farnham, Ross Fraser and David

Hirschfelder in the studio, as they made up the numbers, while 'Let Me Out' was written by Farnham and Hirschfelder. With the possible exception of 'One Step Away', the album doesn't really contain any straight-out pop songs. Mostly, they had 'good lyrics' that were aimed at an adult contemporary audience and they had something to say. It is also possible to see a theme running through the lyrics of a number of the songs, a recurring invocation of independence that one is tempted to associate with the personal motivation behind the production of the album itself. Farnham has been quoted as saying that 'You're the Voice' is 'basically about being master of your own destiny' (Sutton 1986) and that is certainly what *Whispering Jack* enabled John Farnham to be from then on. It is probably appropriate that 'You're the Voice', over time, has come to stand in for the whole album in popular memory, because its theme of personal integrity and social responsibility informs a few of the songs – and indeed, it also flows over into some of the songs on the follow-up album, *Age of Reason* (1988) (such as the title track), and its successor, *Chain Reaction* (1990) (such as 'That's Freedom').

The 'good beats', and how they are created, are a real feature of the album. As was relatively common among many of their international contemporaries – Duran Duran, Depeche Mode, Orchestral Manoeuvres in the Dark, Thomas Dolby – the team producing *Whispering Jack* did without a live drummer and, except for two tracks, a bass guitar (Roger McLachlan plays a fretless bass on 'You're the Voice' and 'A Touch of Paradise'). Influenced by a number of the new wave synthesizer bands of the 1980s, they explored the capacities of the new technologies available to see what they could do. On many of the tracks, this involved setting up a percussion pattern with an electronically manufactured sound (the 'maracas' on 'Pressure Down', the reprocessed handclaps on 'You're the Voice', the exotic-sounding percussion on 'A Touch of Paradise'), and then progressively adding more layers, usually including a strong bass line, gradually injecting more beats and colour into the rhythm track. The drum formats tended towards the epic, with huge, reverbed drum effects on many of the tracks. The bass parts were played on keyboards by Hirschfelder, and synthesizers were often used as a rhythm instrument as well as laying down melodic and harmonic themes, chord progressions and fills.

These good beats, then, were not only generated from Fraser's drum machines, but they were also products of what Hirschfelder calls his 'mock orchestra', the sophisticated orchestration he described as fundamental to the album's ambition. Indeed, it is the breadth and depth of the soundscape that Hirschfelder paints for the album that is among its most remarkable qualities ('he's a genius', says Brady, 'an incredible musician', says Fraser), with a distinctive musical vision elaborated for every song. What is achieved via Hirschfelder's mock orchestra is on another level, creatively, to what the standard soft-rock backing band ordinarily sets out to achieve. Much of this, of course, is also down to Ross Fraser's skill in pulling all this together. By Australian standards of the time, this was a state-of-the-art production, complex and detailed (Nimmervoll 2004: 153). Apter (2016b) refers to the album being 'produced to within an inch of its life', but this seems to me as rather a snarky way of recognizing how accomplished and inventive Ross Fraser was as a producer. The keyboards and drum machines in particular are involved in generating many layers of sound at once, but the production consistently manages the complexity without burying them in the mix. Fraser and Doug Brady worked together on the mix, sitting side by side ('it took a long time' Fraser says), with Farnham dropping in from time to time to listen and make comments. Hirschfelder points to the technical skills of their sound engineer (Doug Brady was only twenty-one at the time and this was his first big job) in bringing sounds in and out of the mix. Brady, says Hirschfelder, had 'great technical understanding of how to emphasise and de-emphasise certain frequencies', 'experimenting [with] putting different instruments, different keyboards, and parts of the vocals through different effects to give them their own space in the mix', and Brady himself describes the process in similarly spatial terms. The result is an exceptional clarity in the separation of the tracks, notwithstanding the number of components in the mix. In the recording studio, they used two twenty-four track digital machines, so there were forty-eight tracks available to them. Even so, says Brady, 'they were chockers!' and they wound up using another twenty-four tracks delivered 'live' from the Fairlight CMI at the mixing stage.

Finally, and to return to Hirschfelder's description, the ambition of harnessing 'the energy of rock' seems to have been thoroughly fulfilled. Not only is the album full of the beats that would 'move audiences' on the dance floor, but it is also continually resonating with its rock heritage: the swampy funk of the bass line in 'Love to Shine', the over-the-top lead guitar on 'Let Me Out', the sassy sax solo on 'One Step Away', the raspy shouty vocals on 'Let Me Out' and more. And then, of course, there is its direct engagement with the prevailing international trends within rock and popular music of the moment: from the expanding role of keyboards and electronic technologies, to the creation of big, complex, highly produced soundscapes, to the specific echoes of particular sounds and techniques that we can hear at various points which recall some of the mainstream acts of the 1980s – for me, that includes Phil Collins, the Eurythmics, Robert Palmer and Peter Gabriel.

The 'whiz-bang' album

It is that engagement with electronics, and perhaps the centrality of keyboards, that may have been the most surprising aspect of the album when it came out. Producer Ross Fraser was the one who raised the possibility that they could do something different, using Hirschfelder's synthesizer, the Fairlight, drum samples and so on. Farnham was definitely 'up for that' and consequently, Fraser says, there are a lot of 'firsts' on the album: 'basically', he says, 'we were doing an electronic album'. Apter quotes Ross Fraser saying that he had been 'dying to do a high-tech album, lots of computers, drum machines'. He wanted 'to take all these tacky machines and put it together in some sort of whiz-bang album. So did John'. (Apter 2016b: 144). Hirschfelder was all in favour as well, and the final member of what became the four-person team once they moved into their collaboration in the studio, Doug Brady, says he, too, was 'into synths and samplers, all that sort of thing'. So while this may not have been the album that those in the industry nor those among Farnham's existing fan base might have expected from John Farnham, this is the album they all really wanted to make.

Numerous reports suggest that Farnham had approached *Whispering Jack* as the album where he would finally get to record the music he most wanted to play, and the way he wanted to play it. As Hirschfelder describes it, and this is supported by the two most recent biographies (Apter 2016; Gazzo 2015), Farnham had decided: 'I'm just gonna do the album I want to do.' There had been some hints of what this might sound like, Hirschfelder also suggested, in the Little River Band album, *Playing to Win* (1985). Both Farnham and Hirschfelder had worked on that album; they were on similar pages in terms of their musical interests and tastes, and were keen to work together as that formation of LRB was being wound up during 1985. Both were interested in pursuing technical and artistic experimentation in the studio. According to Hirschfelder, there were no real expectations that this would help them achieve commercial success, although the popular media narrative around this tells it slightly differently: as outlined in Chapter 1, the standard backstory has Farnham depending on *Whispering Jack* as the catalyst for a revival of his solo career. Whatever their expectations might have been as they worked on the project, however, there is no doubt that Farnham, Fraser and Hirschfelder were committed to exploring the new technologies which were extending what could be done in the studio, and to producing something that was up-to-the-minute, distinctive and special. This was not going to be business as usual.

In terms of who might have been their models for such a project, Hirschfelder made some interesting observations about the musicians to whom they had been paying attention at the time. Farnham had been listening to Peter Gabriel, for example, and he had been a long-time fan of Stevie Wonder. Not only were they both interesting as singers, but they were also early adopters of the Fairlight CMI; indeed, the Fairlight had featured in a famous performance by Stevie Wonder, Herbie Hancock, Thomas Dolby and Howard Jones at the 1985 Grammy Awards.[1] Perhaps surprising (at least, to me) was Hirschfelder's revelation that both Farnham and himself were fans of progressive rock (Hirschfelder mentioned King Crimson as a favourite for him, and Yes, for Farnham). More particularly, Fraser says he was influenced by much of the contemporary music coming out of the UK, particularly the Thompson Twins and, like both Hirschfelder and Farnham, by Tears for Fears' 1985 album, *Songs from the Big Chair*. This album included two big international hits: 'Everybody Wants to Rule the World' and 'Shout' and, Hirschfelder says, it was a 'big production record with big drum sounds, lots of guitars, big reverb – huge'. He also mentioned the 'shiny brassy keyboard sounds' of Go West, but the second British album which seemed to have most attracted him and Farnham was the 1983 album by Yes, *90125* which included the hit 'Owner of a Lonely Heart'. Hirschfelder describes that album as 'big production rock, slightly progressive, a bit edgy but very melodic' – itself not a bad description of what *Whispering Jack* became. The Yes album, with its mainstreaming shift from the band's earlier 'art-rock' history, does seem like a particularly relevant point of reference for the kind of orchestration used on *Whispering Jack*. In general, then, the bands that both Fraser and Hirschfelder mentioned in this context foregrounded synthesizers and other keyboards, generating a big, highly produced, soundscape behind strong melodies and reverbed vocals.

Even though it is suggested that the keyboard successfully dislodged the guitar as the sonic centrepiece of the rock band during the 1980s (Lenhoff and Robertson 2019), it is important to note that the increasing use of electronically manufactured sounds was not universally welcomed. There were concerns that live musicians were being replaced, that there was something ersatz or inauthentic about the electronic sound, that the specific character of individual instruments was being lost, and that the music which resulted from the widespread take-up of the synthesizer in particular was becoming too perfect, almost non-human (Gunders 2012; Hayward 1992c). Significantly, 'robotic' was the word critics commonly used to characterize the performances of one of the earliest exponents of electronic, synth-based, music, the German band, Kraftwerk (a characterization that was only reinforced by Kraftwerk releasing a single called 'The Robots' in 1978). Hirschfelder was clearly sensitive to these issues at the time, and both he and Brady discussed with me the efforts the *Whispering Jack* team made to ensure they retained the human element in the album, by partially resisting making full use of the degrees of precision made possible by the new technologies. Rather than going for the kind of quantising that lines up its sounds perfectly on a grid, they went for a 'soft quantising' allowing for imperfections to 'maintain the personality', and giving it that 'human dimension' to avoid sounding 'too clinical'. Brady noted how meticulous Hirschfelder was in ensuring that nothing was too perfect, even manually 'staggering the notes' to create the dynamics they wanted.

It is worth noting, as a general point, that this seems to have been an exceptionally collaborative creative process between Farnham, Fraser, Hirschfelder and their engineer Brady. The interviews all reinforced that perception. (It is visible even in the album's liner notes which not only list Jack, Ross and Dave against, for instance, the Fairlight and Drum programmes on 'Pressure Down' but also list 'Thelotofus' in 'One Step Away' and 'Everyone' for 'Love to Shine'.) Clearly, the workshopping period with Farnham and Hirschfelder doing the pre-production in Farnham's garage, and with Fraser calling in to participate towards the end of the day (he was also working on another project at the time), was highly collaborative and, it seems, enjoyable. But, as both Fraser and Brady report, the same was true of their experience when they moved into the studio. Both speak highly of the collaboration, in which anyone with an idea to suggest was listened to, and their idea explored. That may well help to account for the imaginative depth of the musical vision that informed the final product, and it also points to the long-term collaborations that followed – Fraser and Brady worked on Farnham's albums for almost thirty years, and for many years Hirschfelder was the musical director for the John Farnham live band before he fully committed to his subsequent career as a film composer.

All of that said, the standout attribute above all in *Whispering Jack* is, of course, John Farnham's voice, and there is quite a bit we need to say about that. Notwithstanding the richness and detail of the album's production, its multi-layered rhythm tracks, its arena-ready melodies and Hirschfelder's extraordinary orchestration, it is Farnham's singing, always at the centre of the mix, that remains its most memorable component.

The voice

In the John Farnham Collection in the National Film and Sound Archive's online exhibition, there is a short television clip from the *Don Lane Show* from 1980, in which John Farnham performs Dan Hill's sentimental ballad, 'Sometimes When We Touch', receiving a standing ovation from Don Lane and his guest, Sammy Davis Jr, and enthusiastic applause from the studio audience. Sammy Davis Jr is clearly impressed by the performance, and takes something of an interest in the young singer – taking over the interview to ask Farnham about his plans for the future. In a moment that says something about Farnham's ambition to move beyond the role of the 'all-round entertainer', Farnham says that he just wants 'to sing'. Pressed further, and with Don Lane telling Sammy Davis Jr in the background how successful Farnham had been as a musical comedy performer, Farnham says that currently he doesn't feel that he does 'any one thing well', and that is why he wants to concentrate on his singing. Sammy Davis Jr, to the appreciative laughter of the audience, assures him that he certainly does sing 'well'. In another TV interview the same year, this time promoting his just released album, *Uncovered*, Farnham tells his interviewer (LRB's Glenn Shorrock, as it happens, filling in for the regular host, Mike Walsh) that this album is a 'little more rock 'n' roll' (although the song he performs on the show,

Graham Goble's 'Please Don't Ask Me', is quite a way from that) and says that he is keen to do more 'contemporary' material in the future. It may have taken six years for these ambitions to fully bear fruit in *Whispering Jack*, but the comments suggest that the intention to pursue a career as a contemporary rock singer was at the front of Farnham's mind at the time.

In the intervening years, his concentration on his singing ended up being transformative: the singer on *Whispering Jack* is a different performer from what had gone before. Studio engineer, Ernie Rose, who had worked on *Uncovered*, told Jane Gazzo that Farnham's stint with LRB may have been helpful in the development of his singing: 'I reckon he learnt a lot about discipline [while working with LRB], he learnt a lot about oversinging' (Gazzo 2015: 184). Oversinging is a way of describing an excessively embellished form of singing, the use of 'vocal gymnastics' that end up dominating the music being performed. Some performers have made an art out of this kind of overly melismatic delivery and have successfully exploited it to the point where it becomes an influential and much-copied vocal style – think Whitney Houston, or even Stevie Wonder. If this was in fact a problem for Farnham as a singer around this time, Rose is probably correct to suggest that working with an established rock band, and in particular a band with such a tight vocal and harmonies dimension as LRB, would certainly have demanded a highly disciplined delivery, and a different kind of delivery to that required in, for instance, the cabaret venues that Farnham had often worked in prior to his recruitment to LRB.

At the time that *Whispering Jack* was under development, Hirschfelder observed that Farnham had been 'experimenting with a much edgier version of his voice'. That's the voice we get on the album, and the difference is particularly noticeable in the handling of his vocal tone, and in his more selective exploitation of his apparently limitless range. There is a raw, raspier edge in his lower and middle register, while in the upper register, rather than attempting to maintain a silky smoothness as he strains for reach, on *Whispering Jack* we have a rock singer 'letting loose' as Brady described it to me, happy to be heard pushing at the edges. What Roland Barthes (2010; 1981) called 'the grain of the voice' has changed; it is a little grittier, it is fuller, not nearly as pretty, and it has gained in the warmth of emotion it can carry. Interestingly, while it sounds more relaxed, it is also deployed in a highly disciplined, more strategic, manner. Fraser contributed to that discipline by encouraging the singer to hold back a little in his delivery, bringing things 'one step down' and leaving those high notes till towards the end of the track, for instance, at which point he could 'go nuts'. The pitch of the songs on *Whispering Jack* is generally lower than was the case on *Uncovered*, so Farnham is using his upper register a little less with the consequence that he has a wider range of tone available to him. What is clear is that every one of his performances on this album commands attention, from the haunting ballad 'A Touch of Paradise' to the stadium rock of 'You're the Voice' or 'Reasons'. Farnham certainly 'sings well', really well, on *Whispering Jack*, but he also rocks. And there is a new sense of authenticity about these vocal performances. In the end, not only is the voice on *Whispering Jack* an extraordinarily versatile and powerful instrument, but it is also simply a better fit with the down-to-earth persona that Farnham had always inhabited. What's more, it sounds like he is enjoying himself. Listening to *Whispering Jack*, it feels like John Farnham had finally found his own voice.

So, let's play the album

I don't want to simply replicate the task of the record reviewer in this section, but it does seem essential to give each track its due in such an extended treatment of the album as this book allows. In doing this, however, I should admit that there are times in what follows when readers will certainly notice that my personal taste and preferences are in play. Music working as it does, one can't pretend that one's responses do not have a personal dimension. I have accepted that it is impossible to totally avoid this if I am to give my account of how the album works, and to point to the elements that have attracted most of my attention. So, with this consumer advice warning in mind, and in the understanding that my responses do not necessarily need to align with those of every other listener, now read on.

The opening track, 'Pressure Down', seems like a statement of intent. It begins with a percussive shuffle, sounding a little like maracas (although, with this album, there is almost no point in trying to identify how the sound being sampled started out!). Then, we have Farnham's 'Oh yeah', which places him right on centre stage, standing in front of a rock band. The big fat rhythmic riff comes in next, with the bass, drums and the synthesizer all working together. A notable feature of the album as a whole is present in this track – (what sounds to me like) the blending of the bass line with parts of the drum format so that it comes across for much of the track as one sound.[2] What we have as a result is something that was certainly innovative at the time, a percussion sound that plays notes as well as beats. As we move into the bridge that bass sound changes slightly – now it sounds more like a woody fretless and it is audible on its own. Around all of this the synthesizers do their melodic fills while maintaining their presence in the rhythm phrase that drives the song; and one of the keyboards comes in to deliver a soaring solo after the bridge. Farnham's vocals start out warm and relaxed, allowing the song to build, and singing his own harmonies. The chorus is held back until after the second verse, but when it finally arrives it is infectious, melodic and delivering those 'good beats' while pushing that message of independence noted earlier: 'Take hold of the wheels, turn them around /Take the pressure down.' The track builds rapidly from there, with Farnham performing his trick of leaping up an octave for the final three choruses. Remarkably, he is still able to pull off the high harmonies despite the leap in pitch. 'Pressure Down' is an arresting opening track that sets the direction for what is to follow – something that really *is* 'a little more rock 'n' roll'.

What comes next is the album's killer song, 'You're the Voice'. There is good reason for this song to have moved audiences over so many years. The beginning of the track has one of the great openings for a rock song, teasing and dramatic. First, we have the reprocessed handclaps setting up their signature percussion pattern, then the piano and drums introduce some colour, followed by the (live) fretless bass adding a great melodic fill that sets up the introduction of the first of the synthesizers, gradually swelling the soundscape before the second synth comes in. Then the vocals begin. There are lots of stories about the vocals on this track; apparently, they were recorded in a couple of takes on the very last day in the studio because Farnham was unhappy with what he had produced so far. It is hard to imagine how anyone could sing this any better. The control of tone and phrasing is remarkable, as the singer moves into falsetto at times before belting out a full-throated rock star delivery of the lines that lead us into the chorus: 'how long/ can we look at each other/through the barrel of a gun.' There is a massive Phil Collins-style drum fill before we hit what must be one of the most sung choruses ever. The synth adds a drone effect under the chorus that prefigures the bagpipe solo to come later, and Farnham is moved back slightly in the mix to blend into the reverbed voices of the back-up singers. This is getting huge, but then we move into the bagpipes solo. Apparently a nightmare to mix (Doug Brady says that getting the pitch right was so difficult they had to mix the drone and the chanter separately), their insertion works brilliantly. The bagpipes not only generate the stirring effect that is entirely consonant with the song's message, but they also recall AC/DC's classic use of the bagpipe solo in their 'Long Way to the Top'. Underneath all of this the handclap percussion pattern persists, refusing to allow the song to drag or lose any of its energy. (Fraser has noted that the first American remix of the song removed the handclaps, to the great detriment of the song's overall effect and it had no success in the United States; a later version, with the handclaps back in, made it to No. 1 in seven states [Adams 2018].) The close-out is epic, with the layered contributions from the bagpipes, the drone motif from the synth, Garsed's guitar getting increasingly frenetic as it proceeds but still some way back in the mix, the reverbed back-up vocals and the big drum fills all in there. As Hirschfelder said, this is where Brady's skill is most critical: there is a mass of content in here, it all works together, and it is all audible to the careful listener. And, of course, it should be said that this is just a great song, with an irresistible chorus; it is surprising that no one had picked it up to record earlier than this.

'One Step Away' has the challenging task of following 'You're the Voice'. Written by Jon Kennett and Dave Skinner, it is the only song on the album, in my view, that works like a traditional pop song in that it is solely organized around its hook – the chorus line, 'One step away / From your love'. Lyrically, there is not much more to it than that hook – hence Apter's comment that the song was 'a piece of lightweight fluff that could have been lifted straight from the Huey Lewis and the News songbook' (2016a: 160). That is overly harsh, however, even though Apter acknowledges that Farnham's vocals end up lifting the track. 'One Step Away' is slightly atypical of the approach taken in the rest of the album as it hits its straps straight away with jangly chords from the synths and guitars, and with the introduction of a throbbing bass line which works busily through the chord progression and ends up giving the track its energy. The vocals are heavily reverbed and this is one of the tracks where that edgier and more soul-influenced voice comes to the fore, with Farnham stretching out as the track builds. There are other memorable features, too, which lift the track: Bill Harrower's soulful sax solo, Brett Garsed's guitar fills and the mischievous insertion of the occasional *Shaft*-like effects into the percussion tracks. This last feature is an example of something that keeps happening with this album: the discovery of the random things that emerge when a creative team in the studio has the freedom to 'muck around' with sound.

Sam See's song 'Reasons', the fourth track, is a good example of the layered approach noted earlier in this chapter. It begins with a strong syncopated bass line using a slightly guttural electronically manufactured sound. That sound alone is enough to grab your attention but the bass line ends up driving the track throughout. Chiming chords from the synthesizer come over the top of this, together with a two-handed keyboard rhythm fill. Then the vocals. The lyric in this song is an interesting one, with the verses in particular presenting a distinctive take on the theme of finding a purpose and direction – the 'reasons' of the title. There is space to take in the lyric, as the song gives us two verses before leading us into the bridge. More layers of percussion are added on the way, along with piano, and one of the synths starts to play the bass line as well, so that its part in driving the song is strengthened. The bridge follows the two verses, taking us on a gradual riser until we finally hit the chorus. There, the big echoing drum sounds dominate, used in conjunction with (what sounds like) handclaps to punctuate each line of the chorus. By this time we have a highly layered rhythm track setting up a complicated set of beats that augment what is happening with the melody. The end of the track takes us back to where we began, with the layers falling off around that wonderful bass line which plays us out. The memorable character of 'Reasons' comes not only from its thoughtful lyric, nor only from Farnham's vocals, nor from what is actually a very strong melodic core, but also from the effect of these multiple rhythms. It's hard not to move in response to it.

Track five is 'Going, Going, Gone', written by Farnham, Fraser and Hirschfelder. According to Hirschfelder, this was one of two songs written to fill the gap in material they encountered as they were selecting songs. It's not the strongest song on the album, and it does tend towards the pop song model in its dependence on the hook in the title for its structure. But there is more to it than that. In fact, it is tempting to read the lyric as having an autobiographical relevance. The chorus, goes: 'Going, going, gone, don't wait too long/You can't hold on if you're too far gone/ Going, going, gone, the pressure's on/ Don't wait too long before you're too far gone.' Given the career context in which this was written, it does seem apposite. The song is the first on the album to foreground Garsed's guitar, not only in the big opening chords but also in the lead break. It is also notable for the use of the brass samples on the chorus and in the slightly chaotic instrumental break. The vocals are pitched higher than most other tracks on the album, double tracked and heavily reverbed, and Farnham gives it both barrels. It is then a likeable track that derives its appeal from the energy of the vocals, and the freshness generated by those brass samples.

Almost as soon as 'Going, Going, Gone' is done, the bass line for 'No One Comes Close' cuts in, and takes us into another musical genre, that of romantic blue-eyed soul. Written by Mondo Rock's Eric McCosker, the lyric in 'No-One Comes Close' is an almost wistful lament, that deals with an 'old flame's' attempts to 'get free' of his former lover, who is now a public figure – 'I see you in those up market movies/You talk on the talk shows. I stare at the TV.' Musically, though, it is a little tougher than that, starting out with the woody bass sound right in the front of the mix, not only setting up the bass line but also the key melodic figure that will run throughout the song. Joined by shiny keyboards, it manages to be both funky and creamy smooth at the same time. The vocals are especially remarkable, warm, up close and fully channelling the song's emotion. Farnham is pulled back into the mix for the chorus, before he finally stretches out into soul singer mode as the song builds around the repeated cries of 'free of you/ free of you', towards the end. The effect of these vocals is an intimate one, and the song delivers quite an emotional punch through them. Underneath it all, the bass and keyboards strut together through a melodic progression of chords in ways that remind me of the kinds of things we heard after Michael McDonald joined the Doobie Bros: something like an alternative melodic line played by the bass and keyboards, just cooking along under the song's main melody. A cool and dreamy guitar solo from Brett Garsed completes the arrangement. It is probably time to acknowledge here that it is easy to overlook the quality of Garsed's contributions to the album, as the orchestration is so layered and so dominated by the keyboards, and given how much attention is inevitably focused on Farnham's vocals, but this is just another one of those moments when what Garsed does is precise, economical, clever and skilful.

By the time we hit the following track, 'Love to Shine', co-written by Kiki Dee and Harry Bogdanov, Hirschfelder's performance on the bass has become one of the real highlights of the album. It is hard for a mere listener to imagine precisely how this is being done on a keyboard, rather than on a stringed instrument, but there is more than his technical expertise involved. This is primarily about musical vision. What is most striking for me is Hirschfelder's frequent use of the bass as, in effect, a lead instrument: it delivers structuring bass lines, melodic fills, and works closely not only with the drums but also with the other keyboards. On 'Love to Shine', there is a brief set of chords from the synth before the bass hits you loud and clear with a swampy, partly syncopated, intro. Given a woody fretless sound similar to the previous track, the bass is even more important here – driving the track along rhythmically, performing the fills between lines, and multiplying the beats. Farnham's vocals on this track are probably the most impressive on the album, in my opinion. They are warm and close at first but then climbing in intensity as the song progresses, until he makes that leap into his upper register to deliver a full rock star finale. Listening to this, one wonders why anyone could ever have questioned his credibility as a rock singer. The sound achieved for the chorus from backing singers Venetta Fields and Sherlie Matthews is straight southern gospel, and compelling. This is an interesting choice of style for what could be read as a relatively straight romantic lyric, or alternatively it could be seen to have something of a spiritual element in it: 'I want our love to shine, down on me/Shining down from up above/ You are part of me.' The gospel overtones to the production generate an uplifting, inspirational element that fits well with the song whichever way it is read. In a contribution that adds a further tonal dimension to the song's arrangement, Garsed's gnarly guitar sound cuts in following the bridge, disrupting the melody of the chorus line before working its way into longer, cleaner and more melodic lines by the time it lifts us back into the verse.

I'll admit that this is my personal favourite on the album, this powerful combination of Memphis/New Orleans funk and the gospel-style chorus that forces you to get up out of your seat. What is particularly impressive, given what we know about the electronic production process, is how the track builds momentum and power, with the bass pushing at us ever more insistently and Farnham's vocals continually raising the temperature. We noted earlier the contemporary concerns about the suggested limitations of electronically manufactured music, but there is nothing 'clinical' or 'non-human' about this. It sounds for all the world as if it was performed live by a real live band. And, in a sense, I guess it was, just not in the way we might previously have understood it.

The emotional temperature gets dialled back down for 'Trouble', although there is no reduction in rhythm or fun. Written by South African singer and songwriter Dennis East, it double tracks Farnham's vocals, and makes a little more use of the guitar in the foundation of the track. There is an infectious bass (there's that woody bass sound again) and a drum pattern that has more of a pop aesthetic than most of the other tracks on the album – with maybe a nod to the Eurythmics. Farnham's vocals are once again a feature, and another sizzling guitar solo from Brett Garsed gives the track some real bite, but the highlight for me on this track is the way the female voices on the chorus are used. For a start, the first two lines of the chorus are completely handed over to the back-up singers, Nikki Nicholls and Penny Dyer, and they have been given a particularly 1980s pop sound, which to me recalls Madonna's

'Material Girl'. It is very different to the sound of the other back-up vocals on the album: no big reverb, but rather a relatively flat mix with the female voices fully in the foreground. As a result, the chorus dances along in a really enjoyable way, refreshing the sound palette used in the album so far.

What comes next is even better. Starting with the distinctive but spare beats, the opening chords establishing a fittingly exotic feel, 'A Touch of Paradise' uses the mesmeric repeated synth chords to build a haunting, romantic soundscape. It is a good example of the way that Hirschfelder layers his keyboards to create atmosphere as well as harmonies around the song's melody. It's a wonderful song, with its opening lines creating quite a picture: 'Flamingoes walk, and sway in peace/ Seeing this, it makes my trouble cease/ The sun is hiding, leaving a pink scar/ That stretches right across the sky/ That's all we've seen so far.' Written by Ross Wilson and Gulliver Smith, the original version, recorded by Mondo Rock and sung by Ross Wilson, is itself impressive but the *Whispering Jack* version does take it to another level. There is some serious keyboard firepower in play here, with layered synth and Fairlight sounds swelling as the song progresses, leading into an atmospheric, but slightly distant, sax solo. Even though this arrangement actually follows the original quite faithfully, it benefits from a clearer conception of just what constitutes the strength of the song's melody, and how to foreground its qualities. While the arrangement is lush, it is also relatively discreet about just how prominent it wants to be – much of what it achieves is done by suggestion. The star is Farnham's singing, enhanced with a touch of reverb, which focuses more clearly on the job of delivering the song's melody than Wilson does in the original (although, I should add, there is nothing wrong with Wilson's version). What is especially notable, for me, are the back-up vocals, from Nikki Nicholls and Penny Dyer again. While they are some way back in the mix, there is a clear separation between each of them, so you can actually hear and appreciate the beauty of each of those voices. That makes quite a contribution to the success of the track's construction of its mood, in my view, as well as its musical pleasures.

The last track, 'Let Me Out', is written by Farnham and Hirschfelder, and it has Farnham in full rock shouter mode, with hard-edged vocals, given lots of reverb (even some echo). Unlike the rest of the album, this track is not so much about the melody – it is all about the rhythm, foregrounding the drum format in the splashy fills that work as an integral part of the song's structure once it hits the chorus. The lyric is an angry one, and the arrangement faithfully reflects that with its aggressive sound palette – the pushy brass fills, the Phil Collins-style drum sound, the shouting vocals, and Brett Garsed's action-packed, slightly over-the-top guitar solo. This is the closest thing to a hard-rock performance on an album that might otherwise be classified overall as soft-rock, notwithstanding its infectious rhythms. 'Let Me Out' demonstrates, convincingly in my view, Farnham's ability to deliver a strong performance in that territory. That said, because the style adopted for 'Let Me Out' does run slightly against the grain of the rest of the album, to my ears it does bring the album to a slightly dissonant end. Maybe that is one reason why the 2006 CD reissue included an extended and quite different version of 'Pressure Down' as a new, additional final track.

That's the album then, and as would be clear from these comments, there are many standout tracks on what remains an immensely satisfying album to listen to, to move to or to sing along to, more than three decades after it was produced. Some tracks have become, in their way, Australian 'classics' – and in the following chapter, I am going to deal in a little more depth with one of them, 'You're the Voice'. It is little wonder that the album was so successful in rebooting Farnham's career. He emerges from *Whispering Jack* as a supremely talented and skilful singer, with the ability to deliver emotionally as well as musically. Hirschfelder, too, with such an extensive hand in the album's sounds and arrangements, demonstrates the scale and quality of his musical vision – his contribution to the album's achievement is immeasurable. And finally, the choice to take on a relatively inexperienced producer in Ross Fraser also paid off in spades, in the form of one of the most polished and inventive albums to emerge from the local industry. That it has sold into roughly one in five Australian households (that's one estimate of its currency) is a testament to how well Fraser did his job, and how well it has lasted.

Timeless

'Reaction' videos are among the niche mini-genres to have become popular online via YouTube in recent years; they record a listener's reaction to a piece of music they are hearing for the first time. In March, 2021, Jamel AKA Jamal posted his reaction to the original 1986 video of *Whispering Jack*'s 'You're the Voice'.[3] He was most impressed. 'This', he said, 'is the very definition of timeless music', that is just as powerful 'if you play it today' as it must have been when it was first released. This certainly seems to be the case. While, as a concept and a production, *Whispering Jack* was firmly located at the leading edge of what were the dominant sounds of the 1980s, as a completed piece of music out there in the market continually finding new audiences for thirty-five years, it has enjoyed an extraordinary longevity. Let us conclude this chapter, then, by considering some of the ways in which the album, and indeed its influence on the industry, have lasted.

In early 1987, Farnham took his band on the road to promote the new album, but since no one had been expecting the scale of the success it was to enjoy they were initially booked into smaller venues, and pubs located in the outer suburbs. In some of these venues, they had trouble fitting all their gear onto the stage (particularly Hirschfelder's suite of keyboards). It soon became clear that these venues couldn't handle the scale of the audience interest either – there were long queues of punters around the block waiting to get in everywhere they went. By the time the tour was half way over, the promoters were looking to secure bookings for additional gigs at major stadiums such as Melbourne's Rod Laver Arena. Once they had moved to the larger venues, the original six-piece band was expanded and they added a brass section. This immediate audience response to the 'Jack's Back' tour suggests that there was a large fan base out there, just waiting for this album; maybe it wasn't the album they were expecting but Australia was certainly ready for the reinvention of John Farnham. The following year, the 'Classic Jack' tour was even bigger, conducted in partnership with a ten-piece mini-version of the

Melbourne Symphony Orchestra, and there were similar, and even bigger, partnerships with other major music companies and institutions to follow in the future. Over the following years, John Farnham continued to fill the largest arenas in the country, and even when he retired from full-scale touring, he could still mobilize his audience around special events (such as the 'Two Strong Hearts' tour with Olivia Newton John in 2015). In his account of one such performance from 2015 at the Sydney Entertainment Centre, Jeff Apter (2016a: 281) notes that, at the time of his writing, Farnham had filled that arena (which has a capacity of 12,000) a total of 77 times over his career.

Whispering Jack produced four hit singles, as well as topping the album charts over 1986–7 and again in 1988. It initiated a series of hit albums for Farnham over the next two decades: *Age of Reason* (1988), *Chain Reaction* (1990) and *Romeo's Heart* (1996): numerous 'greatest hits' collections starting with *Anthology 1* in 1997; live albums and collaborations with other singers including Olivia Newton John, Tom Jones, Human Nature and Jimmy Barnes; as well as more niche projects like the collection of covers of early R&B classics, *33 1/3* (2000). The first three of these albums were particularly important in consolidating the musical brand established with *Whispering Jack* and building the catalogue of hits John Farnham would continue to draw upon in the future. Songs including 'Age of Reason', 'That's Freedom' and 'Burn for You', taken from these albums, became standard inclusions in his live performances. In 2006, a twentieth-anniversary edition of *Whispering Jack* was released, with the extended version of 'Pressure Down' as an additional track, and a concert DVD included. In 2011, the twenty-fifth anniversary of the album's release, Farnham embarked on a national tour performing the album in its entirety and in the original track order. In 2016, Sony released *The Complete Whispering Jack 30th Anniversary* boxset, a limited-edition CD and DVD package which included a thirty-page booklet. If more evidence of the 'timelessness' or longevity of the material on *Whispering Jack* is needed, looking at the most recent concert setlists reveals almost all of the songs from *Whispering Jack* were still there: 'Pressure Down', 'Reasons', 'You're the Voice', 'One Step Away', 'No-One Comes Close', 'Going, Going, Gone' 'Trouble' and 'A Touch of Paradise' were all still being requested and played.

Finally, there is a further dimension to any assessment of the lasting effect of *Whispering Jack*, which is to do with its influence upon the shape of the Australian music industry, an influence that was more extensive than just upon John Farnham's professional career. The success of the 'Jack's Back' tour, which was seen by more than 250,000 fans across Australia and New Zealand, proved that local artists could successfully mount tours that were equivalent in scale to those which had hitherto been led by major international artists. The 1987 tour became the highest-grossing tour ever by an Australian artist, and it did this in competition with tours by Michael Jackson and Billy Joel (Gazzo 2015: 237). Since that time, a select number of other solo artists – Jimmy Barnes, Kylie Minogue, Tina Arena, Delta Goodrem, for instance – have been able to build on that precedent, further confirming the pulling power of arena-ready Australian artists within the local market. This reflects the changing demographics for adult contemporary rock noted in Walker et al.'s account (2012), as it began to address an increasingly broad-based mainstream audience, but within that changing context the success of *Whispering Jack* has had a significant effect, transforming the economics of the music industry in Australia.

Apter (2016b) also suggests the album was influential in generating 'a wave of successful homegrown artists with a "grown up pop" bent', 'everyone from the Rockmelons to Southern Sons, 1927 to Jenny Morris and Peter Blakeley'. He is not alone in this kind of observation; in Ed Nimmervoll's (2004: 153) chapter on the music of 1986, he describes it as 'one of those years when music shifted into another gear'. It is probably no coincidence that 1987 then turned out to be one of the most successful years for Australian artists on Australian charts, as well as for significant international impact. A large number of classic locally produced 'grown up pop' albums came out in that year: Iceworks' *Man of Colours*, James Reyne's first solo album *Motor's Too Fast*, Noiseworks' *Take Me Back*, Jenny Morris's *Body and Soul*, Jimmy Barnes's *Driving Wheels*, Hoodoo Gurus' *Blow Your Cool*, Midnight Oil's *Diesel and Dust*, INXS' *Never Tear Us Apart*, Hunters and Collectors' *What's a Few Men?* and Paul Kelly's *Under the Sun*. It certainly seems likely that the unprecedented scale of the local success of *Whispering Jack*, with its conclusive demonstration that there was a viable mass market for Australian-produced albums in Australia alone, unlocked a few things for Australian musicians, for Australian-based labels and for Australian radio. As the fan website, *I Like Your Old Stuff* remarks in its post on '1987 – The Greatest Year for Aussie Music Ever?' (2017), 'maybe we can blame John Farnham' for all this. That seems a reasonable question to consider.

All of this noted, the special national status earned by just one song, 'You're the Voice', remains as the standout element of the longstanding legacy of *Whispering Jack*, and this is what we will examine in the following chapter.

3 'You're the Voice'

The single of 'You're the Voice' may have just squeaked into the Australian Top 40 (at No. 40) on October 13, 1986, but it only took four weeks to reach No. 1. It also reached No. 1 in Germany and Sweden, No. 6 in the UK and was a major hit in Austria, Switzerland, Ireland, the Netherlands, Canada and New Zealand. According to one of the writers, Chris Thompson, it has been covered at least fifteen times (Adams 2018). The US band Heart had minor success with it in the US and the UK in 1991, and the Greek-language version by Lavrentis Machairitsas was a hit in Greece in 1993. The single stayed on top of the charts in Australia for seven weeks, becoming Farnham's first chart success since the release of 'Help' in 1980, and his first No. 1 since his cover of 'Raindrops Keep Falling on My Head' in 1969. In addition to its chart success, 'You're the Voice' has become something of a popular culture phenomenon in Australia. As we have seen, the song has featured as a key element within numerous events of national celebration over the years, and it has continued to generate enthusiastic participation from audiences wherever it is played. At the time of writing, the most recent example of 'You're the Voice' being performed in such a context was (long-time Farnham fan) Delta Goodrem's rendition at the Anzac Eve 'Music From the Home Front' televised concert on April 24, 2021 (a slightly more downbeat version than Farnham's, and without the signature handclaps).

In recognition of its iconic status, 'You're the Voice' has been made the subject of a separate exhibition within the online collection of materials celebrating John Farnham's seventieth birthday at Australia's National Film and Sound Archive (NFSA). Headlined as a 'tribute to The Voice of Australia', the exhibition contains, among other things, a three-minute video which compiles a composite version of the song by drawing on videos of John Farnham's live performances from the 1980s, 1990s and 2000s. Documenting the song's longevity, it also displays Farnham's shifts in appearance and image as a performer over the three decades. We see the transition from the big blond mullet, the rock star tank top and tanned sweaty arms of the 1980s, through to the more mature and slightly more conservatively coiffed black suit and black shirt of the 1990s, to the tribal elder figure of the 2000s (dark grey suit, white shirt, white tie). (There are no clips in this compilation of Farnham wearing his full-length Drizabone coat onto the stage, unfortunately.) The common element through all the clips, across the three decades, is the level of audience participation: they can be seen joyfully belting out the iconic chorus, standing and doing the wave – joining with Farnham in a collective performance. It's their song well as his, and he acknowledges this as he introduces it in what looks like the earliest clip (judging from the length of his mullet), by saying to the audience, 'thanks for what you have done for this song, I love ya'.

'You're the Voice' was one of the last songs selected for inclusion on *Whispering Jack*. Producer Ross Fraser recounted to me his memory of playing the demo cassette for the first time in his car on the way to Farnham's basement studio; he remembered thinking, 'this is pretty good', smiling at his own understatement. David Hirschfelder also recalled the moment when Fraser played them the demo – 'everyone looked at each other, thinking "John's gonna love this!"' According to Apter's (2016a: 147) account, the song's 'empowering lyric' was something that Farnham 'totally related to and wanted to be identified with. It was a vaguely political song of the people – nothing too overt, but punchy enough when necessary, especially just before the chorus kicked in'. It was written, said Farnham in an interview at the time,

> by four English people: Andy Quinta, who plays with Icehouse; Chris Thompson, who has a solo album out at the moment and was the lead singer with Manfred Mann for ages – he sang 'Blinded By The Light'; Keith Reid, who I found out the other day actually wrote the words for Procul Harum's 'Whiter Shade of Pale'; and a lady named Maggie Ryder, a session singer from England who worked with the Eurythymics for a couple of years. (Sutton 1986)

Reputedly, the idea for the song came when two of the writers, Quinta and Thompson, were watching the 1983 CND march in London's Hyde Park live on TV (Adams 2018).

It is no secret that the path to recording 'You're the Voice' was not smooth. When the writers were approached for their permission, they were initially resistant to the idea of John Farnham recording it (Adams 2018). Chris Thompson was opposed because, as far as he knew, Farnham was 'Sadie the Cleaning Lady': he's 'like a joke in Australia' and so 'there is absolutely no way is he doing that song'. Eventually he agreed to listen to the recording before deciding whether he would allow it to be released: 'If I didn't like it, I could say no.' In the event, Thompson thought it was 'fantastic. They had stuck to the original demo, which is every songwriter's dream. They changed one note on the bass and put in this brilliant bagpipe solo' (eventually, Thompson included the bagpipes in his own live performances of the song) (Adams 2018). And similarly, as we have seen, the path to airplay was fraught for the same reasons. Glenn Wheatley recalls:

> I knew people at radio would still have a problem playing a John Farnham song, they'd still think of it as Johnny Farnham. I had a few stations straight up tell me 'we'd never play a John Farnham song, he's the Sadie man'. So I put it out on a white label without his name on it. But eventually 2DAYFM in Sydney added it, they were the first. And . . . within a week or two it was the most requested song on the station. (Adams 2018)

In addition to these stories, however, which are about the song's road to commercial success, there is also the longer-running story that has 'You're the Voice' becoming something of a national treasure. The NFSA exhibition's contextualizing introduction puts it like this: 'the protest song written by a group of Brits . . . has become one of the most loved and iconic rock anthems in Australian music history. To this day, it has the power to unite a crowd in song'.

Ross Fraser, when I asked him what was so special about the song, observed: 'There are two things about this record. . . . One is the lyric and the other is the musicianship.' We have already discussed the musicianship in Chapter 2, but there is more to say about the power and direction of the lyric. Fraser says: 'It's going to stay there for a very long time. The lyrics mean something *now*, and that was 35 years ago. What we are going through now, there is still war and still famine . . . that song still resonates with a lot of people. . . . It's a serious song, it's a serious song.' The lead in to the chorus – 'we're all someone's daughter/ we're all someone's son/ how long can we look at each other/ through the barrel of a gun' – is a moment of particular resonance, both through the clarity and power of the lyric and through the way that it is foregrounded by the structure of the song. It's a perfect marriage between the music and the lyric, each reinforcing the strength of the other.

The unofficial national anthem

That takes us some way, but it is still remarkable that the song has achieved the status it has within the national culture, as a song that is not only loved and shared but which also appears to speak specifically to Australians. Debbie Kruger (1987) touches on that when she describes 'You're the Voice' as 'the anthem for the Australian spirit'. She implies that there is something about the song's particular message and power that appears to Australians to refer especially to them: a particular homology between the song's political message and longstanding Australian cultural mythologies about the attributes of self-reliance, resilience and egalitarianism embedded in the national character. Farnham says that he himself 'never started calling it a national anthem, it just happened, and it knocks me away every time someone refers to it as that. It's absolutely amazing' (Adams 2018). This must happen a lot, as Farnham also admits that his sons regularly send him recordings of 'You're the Voice' being sung like an anthem in bars, clubs, pubs and football matches (Adams 2018).

It's not just in these locations, either. When Bernard Zuel (2016) was interviewing fans at the John Farnham Band's 'The Last Time' live tour in 2002, he interviewed two friends in their late twenties and early thirties who had seats 'up the front'. When he asked them how long they had been fans, they both said 'since 'You're the Voice', with one of them adding, 'I learnt it at school'. The cultural significance of the song has evidently been understood outside Australia as well. When Coldplay's Chris Martin brought Farnham on to the stage to sing 'You're the Voice' for the Sound Relief concert in 2009 (introducing him as 'the King of Australia'), he described the song, then, as the unofficial national anthem. Another instance of the international currency of this connection is cited in an episode of James Mathison and Osher Günsberg's (2021) podcast, *Idle Australians*, which was devoted to 'You're the Voice'. One of the hosts recalls attending a match at the World Cup of soccer in Germany, in 2006, when Australia famously managed to progress beyond the first round by drawing 2–2 with Croatia. After the final whistle sounded, the PA in the stadium in Stuttgart started playing 'You're the Voice' and 30,000 ecstatic Australians sang along in celebration. Furthermore, it is probably worth pointing out that the song has established a wider, more transnational relevance as well, and has been used around the world on occasion as an anthem of freedom and resistance. When Mathison and Günsberg interview Ross Fraser, he tells them that 'when they knocked down the wall in East Berlin, they were playing "You're the Voice"', a reminder not only that it was hugely successful in Germany but also how the power of that lyric resonated in the most volatile of political contexts. Unfortunately, it is also the case that something like this can be easily appropriated and put to work in unpredictable ways. Farnham understandably objected, for instance, when the song was played by right-wing Reclaim Australia protesters at an anti-immigration and anti-refugees rally in Melbourne in 2018.

Of course, it must be admitted that the popular embrace of the song in Australia has occurred in a country that is not at all in love with its official national anthem, 'Advance Australia Fair', so it is perhaps not surprising that a more grassroots alternative might gain some traction. Indeed, there have been a number of popular contenders for a preferable national song over the years. Peter Allen's sentimental ballad 'I Still Call Australia Home' is capable of rousing an audience to sing along, although this may be related at least partly to the song's appropriation by the national airline, Qantas, for a long-running series of nationalistic television advertisements. Similarly, 'I am Australian', written by Bruce Woodley of The Seekers and Dobe Newton of The Bushwhackers, from time to time, has been proposed as an alternative to 'Advance Australia Fair'. That case has some merit: it, too, is often sung at national events; it has become a standard item on the programme for school choirs and other community performances, and often it has been used in nationalistic advertising – most recently, in promoting ABC television. These are slow ballads, though, which generate a very different, far less exuberant, performance than 'You're the Voice'. They are both slightly nostalgic reflections on national belonging rather than a celebration of contemporary empowerment, and neither of them belong in a rock concert. Other contenders, that would be more comfortable in that context but nonetheless more likely to be sung in pubs than at national events and also less likely to have such broad-based public support, would be Men at Work's 'The Land Down Under', or even (curiously, go figure!) Darryl Braithwaite's cover of Ricki Lee Jones and Walter Becker's 'The Horses'.

So, while there is no shortage of popular songs that can be sung as a means of signifying or celebrating an Australian identity, 'You're the Voice' is the most widely and affectionately regarded of all of these – even though, interestingly, the lyric makes no specific reference to Australia. There are, as noted earlier, the implied links with myths about 'the Australian spirit' that Kruger suggests, but my guess is that the most powerful signifiers of Australia that the song carries are generated by Farnham himself; that is, I am suggesting that the cross-generational national resonance of the song is related to the content of his public persona and to his longevity as a loved Australian performer. It is the public's parasocial[1] relation to Farnham that completes that connection, then, linking the song through him to a broadly shared articulation of particular versions of Australian identity. Glendinning (2002) claims that Farnham is so 'endearing and enduring because he is the embodiment of our national psyche: laidback, easygoing, self-deprecating . . . and fun'. But it's not just the Drizabone coat, or the larrikin persona; it's got to be more complicated than that. In a way, there is a level of affection the Australian public has attached to John Farnham that may come simply from his continued, unassuming, presence and availability in Australians' everyday lives over three decades. You could say that contemporary Australia and Johnny/John Farnham grew up together. As baby boomers such as myself went through our own transitions, we also watched John Farnham grow from the humble, talented but unassuming, nice boy/teen star of the early days, into the (confident but still humble) larrikin, the jokey, self-deprecating virtuoso, nice guy/rock star of his later years. There is a tight fit between these personae and some of the preferred versions of masculine Australian identities of the times in which they grew up.

Over this period, too, the audience for post-punk Australian popular music moved beyond its earlier fragmentation into particular subcultural scenes and taste cultures, towards a more fluid, inclusive and national formation that travelled more easily across demographics and social identities, as well as across what remained of these taste subcultures. It is easy to see how *Whispering Jack* and Farnham himself fitted into this new environment. Also relevant, perhaps, is the fact that his was a success story built entirely within Australia. Running against the grain of so many of the conventional narratives of the path to Australian success – in which success can only be legitimated when achieved overseas – the fact that Farnham built and sustained his career in Australia, demonstrating by his choices that this was enough for him, may well be among the reasons for the affection he inspires in his audiences. There are also larger cultural shifts involved in this story, however, and they are to do with the relationship between Australian popular music and the uprising of cultural nationalism that is such an important component of Australian popular culture during the 1980s, and which contributed significantly to the context that so readily welcomed 'You're the Voice'.

Australian popular music and cultural nationalism

As Marcus Breen's book, *Rock Dogs* (1999; 2006), has laid out, during the late 1970s and 1980s, there was a concerted push within what was then the mainstream of Australian politics to raise the cultural status of popular music. The Hawke Labor government (1983–91) in particular was attracted to the potential of engaging with the popular music industry as a means of tapping into the concerns of the 'youth', the younger members of the Australian electorate who had been conspicuously ignored by the Coalition governments which had preceded Hawke's election in 1983. As Breen notes (2006: 37), a new generation of politicians and activists had emerged during the late 1970s, for whom the experience of popular music had been an integral and important part of their growing up (indeed, Hawke's treasurer and later his successor as prime minister, Paul Keating, had famously once managed a local rock band, The Ramrods). Under the influence of this new generation of political operatives, the Labour Party had come to recognize that 'its electoral success would hinge on an agenda where youth and young people's activities would need to be expressed as part of the policy objectives within the rhetoric of liberal pluralism' (Breen 2006: 24). Over time, what had started out as a cultural and political objective converged with a more economic objective as the international success of popular musicians and bands such as Kylie Minogue, Midnight Oil, INXS, the Little River Band and Men at Work suggested that there was potential for significant export earnings for the industry if it was given appropriate support. Hitherto, popular music had been explicitly excluded from the existing cultural policy and arts industry-funding frameworks, which had focused on supporting elite art forms such as ballet, classical music and fine arts (with some minor attention to community arts). Over the 1980s and into the 1990s, however, support for popular music performers and organizations was progressively integrated into these frameworks through initiatives at both the federal and the state level, leading to significant investments from the federal government (such as the establishment of Ausmusic[2] in 1989) and state governments (such as the Victorian Rock Foundation, launched in 1987).[3] As noted earlier on, there was already broadcasting content regulation in place that provided some protection for local music, but popular music was also taken up as an industry to be supported through training and development initiatives, and by its integration into the growing suite of government-funded programmes devoted to assisting export activity.

It is notable that during this period popular music was increasingly talked about (and indeed thought of itself) as a national cultural formation, notwithstanding the comprehensive internationalization of popular music as an industry that was already in place. As a result, Breen suggests, popular music was one of the more prominent modes of cultural expression that 'helped generate cultural nationalism as part of Australia's social and political discourse of the 1980s' (2006: 54). As my *Making It National: Nationalism and Australian*

Popular Culture (Turner 1994) sets out to demonstrate, cultural nationalism hit something of a peak over this period. This was a time in Australian cultural history when popular culture, across a wide range of its practices and platforms, was enlisted in a process of identity construction and nation formation that was remarkable for its scale, success and its penetration into the national imagination. Rock music was not the only form of expression that was at the leading edge of this – the local film and television industries were very much major players as well – but it was clearly one of the significant influences in generating the meanings of the times and the modes of national belonging that came with them. Indeed, as noted in the Introduction to this book, there was considerable debate, within the industry and among researchers and the arts/music commentariat, about whether we had reached a point where we might have achieved an identifiable 'Australian sound', a local inflection of popular music that could stand alongside such examples as the Motown sound (Breen 2006; Turner 1992), and that spoke of a distinctively Australian experience. As we have seen, pub-rock was often proposed as a candidate for this Australian sound, even though, as I have argued elsewhere (Turner 1992), it might be better understood as a subcultural formation or a set of localized practices and venues rather than the source of an identifiable 'national sound'.

In the end, that debate fizzled out as the tide of cultural nationalism receded, but the fact that it existed at all gives some idea of the part that rock music played in the emerging 'imagined community' that was the Australian nation from the 1980s into the 1990s. Initially, the key points of this cultural nationalism within the music industry were those artists nominated above who had achieved substantial international success. But their success also fed into a more general context where the cultural value of popular music within the experience of Australians' everyday lives (not to mention its potential political value) was more widely acknowledged and understood. The establishment of such a context helps to explain why Farnham was such a significant choice as the Australian of the Year in 1988, the year of the Bicentennial, and why his ongoing career – so much of which was built upon and around the evolving significance of 'You're the Voice' – was to make him a national icon.

Much of what we have been describing here, though, was to change as we headed further into the 1990s, as part of the 'incremental progression of Australian popular music' (Breen 2006: 67). Marcus Breen explains: '[Australian popular music] shifted from a reliance on national symbols with local appeal as in the cases of Men at Work and Midnight Oil, to de-national symbols, where universal ideals like love and emotion were not constrained by local references' (67). On the one hand, this reflected a greater internationalization of the industry's output and its commercial strategies, but on the other hand, this occurred alongside an expansion in the scale and diversity of the local market for recorded music. In 1985, the total dollar value of Australian wholesale music sales was $179 million; by 1990, it was $363 million and by 1995, it had reached $499 million (Breen: 81). While cultural nationalism had receded somewhat from the discursive domain, it does seem to have continued to exercise an influence on the local market as the potential highlighted by the success of *Whispering Jack* was increasingly exploited by local artists aiming at building a major career entirely within Australia. Nimmervoll points out the apparent contradictoriness of this situation in his discussion of the music of 1986. While, he says, 'the Australian music industry kept its eye on the international picture, hoping for more INXS, often stubbornly ignoring contrary local tastes', at the same time 'the two most successful Australian recording artists from here on – John Farnham and Jimmy Barnes – would mean virtually nothing internationally and their fans didn't mind in the least' (2004: 150). So, these two trends – one towards a commercially inspired internationalism, and the other a culturally inspired localism/nationalism – co-existed in ways that supported an expanding music industry into the 1990s despite what might look like their competing commercial dynamics. It is notable that 'You're the Voice' could be cited as an example of either, or both, of these trends with some validity, and that may well be a pointer to the factors underlying its longstanding cultural, as well as its commercial, significance. Viewed from this perspective, it managed to pull off quite a feat.

*   *   *

For popular music to speak in a way that allows it to play a truly national cultural role, its appeal must extend across demographics and social identities, reaching beyond the perimeters of particular localized scenes or taste-based subcultures. One of the more interesting and distinctive things about the United States, for instance, is how popular music is so comprehensively hardwired into its various local and regional cultures on the one hand, but also how much of it is able to communicate nationally, across generations and cultural identities, on the other hand. At its most nationally significant, popular music in America seems uniquely able to represent the nation in sound and to bring its disparate publics together; to a remarkable extent, a great many of America's popular songs have become embedded in the national cultural imagination. I am not sure how much of that kind of integration – between popular music and the national estate – had occurred before (or indeed since) Farnham's performance of 'You're the Voice', but its extraordinary career suggests it must be one of the most dramatic and enduring examples in the Australian context.

4 And then …

Finally, let's conclude by considering what John Farnham has become for the Australian public in the years since the success of *Whispering Jack*: the iconic local hero, the 'uncool' rock star, the much-loved entertainer. To start with, although he might seem like a natural fit for the role of the local hero, John Farnham has never developed anything like the cool persona of the conventional male rock star. As Farnham himself has admitted, 'I don't have a cool bone in my body.' Glenn Wheatley agrees: 'he doesn't try to be cool, he doesn't try to be hip' (Zuel 2016). Rather than being bothered by this, however, Farnham jokes about his failure to be a fashionable figure: 'You're not allowed to say publicly that you own a Farnham album', he says. 'You've got a Farnham album in your hand and it'll be "Yeah I found it on the bus"' (Glendinning 2002). Nonetheless, as anyone who has seen him play live will know, he has become a commanding presence on stage. Rather than this setting him above or apart from his audience, however, he has an almost intimate relationship with them: filling the breaks between songs with blokey banter, a bit of flirting, squeezing hands, kissing the odd baby, responding to requests and cracking the occasional 'dad joke'. Farnham has acknowledged the value of his apprenticeship on the rubber chicken circuit where he learnt to 'work a crowd' – a very different process to negotiating the world of pub-rock but something that has definitely assisted him in creating a connection with his live audiences since then. Farnham says that he 'got bagged' for caring about entertaining his audience 'in the old days' (readers may recall Homan's discussion of the rock music industry's perjorative distinction between the artist and the entertainer outlined in Chapter 1), 'but it is paying off now' (Zuel 2016). Zuel says: 'No other artist I've seen has the connection, the two-way flow of affection and respect between artist and audience. After all, this is a performer who will stop a song just to let someone take a photo' (2016). David Hirschfelder made similar points in our conversation when he expressed his admiration for Farnham's unique connection with his audience, something he witnessed while sharing the stage with him over many years.

The 'ordinary' rock star

So, let's talk about that affection and respect, which arguably has only been consolidated over the years and which constitutes a standard theme within the many retrospectives the media has delivered on his career. Within such media commentary, inevitably, there are any number of attempts to capture the character of Farnham's unique standing with Australian audiences. Examples of such attempts include Glen A. Baker describing him as a 'folk hero, Australia's favourite son' (Gazzo 2015: 339); or Mondo Rock's Ross Wilson, the co-writer of 'Touch of Paradise', suggesting that Farnham's is the 'voice of the common man' (quoted in the introduction to the NFSA online exhibition); or Magda Szubanski, playing the role of 'entertainment reporter Pixie-Anne Wheatley' in the television comedy programme *Fast Forward* in 1991, introducing Farnham for a faux interview as 'the nice guy of rock 'n' roll' (from the NFSA John Farnham video collection). Typically, Farnham's perceived 'Australian-ness' is emphasized as a crucial element. This is invoked in various ways but usually references his unassuming 'ordinariness', his larrikin-like sense of humour, and his familiar 'bloke-iness' (which might be summarized as liking a beer, a smoke and a joke). Australian popular music has always been rooted in the suburbs, but the representation of Farnham in the media results in a kind of proletarianization of popular music stardom: he is modest in aspiration, lacking in pretension, self-deprecating and continually surprised by his success. David Nichols's description is typical when he characterizes Farnham's career as the 'Everyman story of Australian popular music. He's as ordinary as any very wealthy man whose adult life has been largely public can be. Success has also failed to spoil his down-to-earth attitude.' (2017: 545). Journalist Bernard Zuel (2016) has further emphasized this ordinariness by noting the level of stability and consistency Farnham has maintained around his home and working life: 'he has had the same wife for 29 years, the same manager for 23, the same producer and record company for 17. Many of the road crew and band have been with him for more than a decade and tour routines (such as the mandatory one hour run-through every show day) have been the same for years'.

It should be acknowledged here that it is not at all uncommon for media stars, popular musicians, entertainers or celebrities in general to be described in terms which highlight their so-called ordinariness, and for this to be offered up as an endearing, disarming or levelling attribute. Indeed, the active dialectic between the ordinary and the extraordinary is one of the fundamental characteristics which structure the media's construction of all kinds of celebrity. Almost routinely, celebrated public figures are represented as exceptional in terms of their talent or their high levels of visibility (sometimes one or other of those, rather than necessarily both), but they are made more relatable by being depicted as ordinary in terms of their personal lives or the manner in which they present themselves in public[1] (Turner 2014). The difference between someone who is simply a celebrity (i.e. who is merely 'famous for being famous' in Daniel Boorstin's (1971) phrase) and someone who is a talented performer with professional runs on the board, is the degree to which public (i.e. media) interest is focused on their private lives. If they are the former, then the interest in their private lives is paramount and fundamental (think Kim Kardashian); if the latter, then their professional achievements have the capacity to more actively frame and shape how they are known and understood by their publics. In the case of John Farnham, as for Kylie Minogue or perhaps more recently Tina Arena, his public status has shifted significantly over time: from being seen initially as the product of a promotional industry and therefore undeserving of much in the way of professional respect, to a point where his durability and his maturation as a performer have not only sustained the public's interest but also generated affection and respect.

There is nothing 'natural' about this trajectory, however. In the case of all three of these performers, it comes from a determined and long-term commitment to pursue what it is they want to do, or be, as a musician or an entertainer. Significantly, and again in all three cases, the management of their public image has ensured that, by and large and over time, it is their professional careers that have progressively dominated their media presence (more varied, this, for Kylie Minogue, but in general still true). So, what might be hailed as a 'natural' attribute we can recognize in John Farnham the musician, his unaffected ordinariness, must in truth be the result of a great deal of discipline, common sense, good advice, hard work – and a lot of patient resistance to the many temptations to operate more generally as a media personality, and thus become more 'affected'. While this aspect of Farnham's status as a local hero is an important one, then, there is also something slightly patronizing and indeed a little lazy in these 'just an ordinary guy' type of accounts, because they underplay just how difficult it is actually to be your own person when you are in the public eye all the time. Hugely talented as he is, John Farnham is definitely not 'just an ordinary guy', even if there are numerous ways in which he is perceived by his audience, and constructed through the media, as being 'just like the rest of us'.

Further reinforcing such a position, the research I have done for this project, including my interviews with some of those who have worked most closely with him, has continually turned up evidence of the exceptionally high professional standing John Farnham enjoys within the industry itself. Indeed, it seems this was already the case even before the release of *Whispering Jack*. Glen A. Baker (1986b: 77), writing for *Billboard*, describes the general elation in the Australian music industry at Farnham's success with *Whispering Jack*.

He quotes a comment from EMI's head of A&R, Rob Walker, who had worked with Roger Davies on turning Tina Turner's career around with the production of her 'comeback' album *Private Dancer* in 1984: 'There wasn't anybody in the business who didn't want Tina [Turner] to succeed, and it has been the same sort of thing in Australia for John Farnham. There's an indescribable clout, an unstoppable impetus, that comes with the sort of warmth and affection he engenders in people.' As suggested in Chapter 1, Farnham had been 'the singer's singer' for a long time, but without really receiving appropriate industry recognition for his talent. Consequently, when Farnham swept the board at the 1987 *Countdown* national music awards, picking up best-selling Australian album, best single, best album, best male performance in a video as well as the outstanding achievement award, his long-time supporter, the host of television's *Countdown*, Molly Meldrum, said what many in the industry would have been thinking: 'tonight true justice has been done' (*Variety* 1987). In our conversations for this project, Doug Brady told me how he was totally in awe of Farnham when he turned up to work on *Whispering Jack*, while David Hirschfelder tells of his first experience of seeing Farnham perform when he sat in with Kerrie Biddell's jazz band to sing 'Georgia on My Mind': 'this guy could sing *anything*', he thought. And then there is the tribute from guitarist Brett Garsed in his interview on *Live4Guitar*: 'This may sound corny but it's the truth – the fondest memory [of working on *Whispering Jack*] I have is meeting John for the first time and finding out that he's a very generous and respectful bloke with no ego or pretentiousness and is quite simply one of the greatest singers and performers that has ever lived' (Clay 2011).

Garsed is just one of a family of Farnham band members who have been with him for years: Hirschfelder only left the band when he was forced to choose between continuing to tour or to commit fully to what became a major career as a film composer; back-up singers Lisa Edwards, Lindsay Fields and Venetta Fields have been continuing presences over decades as has drummer Angus Birchall. Ross Fraser and Doug Brady have worked on virtually every one of his recording projects since *Whispering Jack*, as well as on live performances and events, with the most recent being the *Two Strong Hearts* live album from the 2015 tour with Olivia Newton John. Fraser and Farnham, at one point, even set up their own record label, Gotham. The longevity of these relationships, and the loyalty they represent, is, to say the least, unusual. Disappointing as all this may be for the more predatory sections of the celebrity and gossip media (or from the more critical end of popular music studies, for that matter), you simply don't come across a bad word about John Farnham. At the risk of labouring the point, that is exceptional, rather than 'ordinary', for a performer in a highly competitive industry within which the star performers are always under the scrutiny of the media and continually exposed to the critical judgement of their audiences.

The Farnham audience

Among the performance clips collected on the NFSA exhibition celebrating Farnham's career is one from 1999, where he and Kylie Minogue are entertaining Australian troops in Dili, East Timor, during the battle for independence in that territory.

These are challenging circumstances, an outdoor concert for soldiers on a makeshift stage in what was effectively a war zone. Farnham works that large and raucous crowd effortlessly, as he knocks out a sizzling performance of 'That's Freedom', to the delight of an enthusiastic audience who would have been in their early teens, at best, when he first revived his career. Among other things, the clip highlights an especially notable aspect of his career: the breadth of the audience he has gathered over the years. Gazzo (2015: 265) has a shot at explaining his broad appeal in her chapter on *Chain Reaction*: 'He was one of the few contemporary performers "nice" enough for mums, "talented" enough for dads, and relevant enough for their kids.' Often, commentary has remarked upon the continuing presence of young fans in his audiences over the decades. The television footage of Farnham's performance at the 2020 Fire Fight concert is just one example where the front of the stage is packed with fans in their teens and twenties, most of whom would have been born decades after *Whispering Jack* was released but who nonetheless know all the lyrics well enough to sing along. However, the original fans have also stuck with him. In 2016 Bernard Zuel republished a 2002 *Sydney Morning Herald* piece which focused on Farnham's broad audience appeal as part of an analysis of the (then) fifty-three-year-old Farnham's 'Last Time' tour. The article highlights the generational spread at that time:

> Coming up the steps are well dressed couples in their 40s, packs of women of indeterminate age, groups of 'mature' citizens and many, many families: boomers and their teenage kids; thirtysomethings and their babies. . . . One woman who

has been coming to see him for 35 years, has brought her daughter this year and only left her mum at home because the venue's steps are getting too much.

This could just as easily have been written about the audience at any of the more recent events as well.

The breadth of Farnham's audience in Australia may have something to do with the important role that television played in building that audience; certainly television provided access to what was potentially a larger and more heterogeneous audience than the pubs attracted, and it provided Farnham with a platform upon which he not only performed his music but through which he also became a familiar personal presence for Australian television viewers. He has been a ratings drawcard for television over the years, from his early roles hosting variety shows and doing guest spots on TV soaps and sitcoms in the 1970s, to his regular appearances on the talk shows of the 1980s and 1990s. In addition, and once his singing career had been rebooted, a number of the concerts and tour events have been converted into television specials. For instance, in an early example from 1987, two concerts were filmed at Melbourne's Sport and Entertainment Centre for a Channel 10 television special. They were state of the art, using new technologies (such as axe-cam, a miniature video camera attached to the bottom of a guitar), and a ten camera setup, including a Steadicam. This was the biggest production of its kind ever mounted in Australia at the time (Tripp 1987), and it was sold internationally as well as being screened nationally.

However, the spread of John Farnham's audience may also reflect the changes to the music market that we discussed earlier in the book. Matt Neal's (2021) account argues that in the 1980s, the music industry was divided into two worlds. On the one hand, there was the mainstream world of 'MTV approved pop and rock stars', the album and single charts and commercial radio, and on the other hand there was 'alternative music' which he describes as a catch-all category that 'covered everything from punk and metal to gangsta rap and indie rock', a 'world of indie labels, low budget recording studios, and van loads of rough and ready bands'. In the United States in the late 1980s, the success of REM was bridging that divide, but it was still solid in Australia, argues Neal, until 1991, when '15 years of post-punk underground rock music finally bubbled over into the mainstream' with the first shots in this 'quasi-revolution' fired by Sydney Indie band Ratcat. Internationally, there was the success of Metallica, Pearl Jam, Red Hot Chili Peppers and Nirvana. The explosion of the divide internationally was manifest when Nirvana toppled Michael Jackson off the US singles charts in 1992, but in Australia it wasn't really until 1994, Neal suggests, that the alt-rock boom 'kicked off in earnest' with Silverchair. I would locate this shift a little earlier in Australia, but in most respects I would agree with Neal's proposed history, and it does have a particular relevance here. Farnham's music on *Whispering Jack* does belong in what Neal describes as a 'mainstream', at a time when 'alternative' was certainly at the other end of the spectrum of cool. But his relaunched career also benefited, as noted earlier, from the gradual evolution of the music world that Neal describes, a world which was becoming less segmented in its taste cultures and audiences, and therefore more ready to welcome a greater diversity of output from a greater variety of performers. The 'mainstream' had just got bigger.

Finally, there is an even more fundamental factor which helps to explain John Farnham's audience appeal, particularly his long-term following. On the back of *Whispering Jack*'s success, Farnham was able to mount live tours that went well beyond what was common in the Australian market at the time. These concerts were major events: the band became a ten-piece outfit once the tour hit the larger venues, with a brass section (mostly), three back-up singers, as well as a continuing cast of familiar personnel, some of whom gathered their own fan base over the years (the live clips, for instance, display the strong audience reaction when Farnham introduces his drummer, Angus Birchall, and back-up singer Lisa Edwards[2]). On some of the tours, the much-respected back-up singer Venetta Fields also performed a short set in the middle of the show. The scale and power of this kind of band explored similar territory to the mega-bands developed by Delaney and Bonney, or Leon Russell's extravaganza surrounding the 'Mad Dogs and Englishmen' tours for Joe Cocker, or the expanded formation of the Doobie Brothers, in the 1970s (a more recent example of this style of concert band would be the Tedeschi-Trucks band). They constituted a significant elevation of what could be expected from a live concert by an Australian-based artist. Furthermore, with the quality of the band, as well as Farnham's performances and showmanship, it is not surprising that these concerts attracted such a crowd, nor that they would be keen to come back for more – again, and again. The size of the crowds attending, as well as the sense of community generated over the years as audiences participated en masse in delivering Farnham's rock anthems, also contributed to the epic, even celebratory, character of these events. That this was usually accompanied by some signifiers of national identity – from the Drizabone coat to Farnham's Aussie banter from the stage or simply the long national career of the songs performed – amplified the sense that this was indeed an essentially Australian celebration, eliciting a palpable sense of belonging. Farnham, of course, stood as the catalyst for these emotions.

As we have seen, there are many 'firsts' associated with *Whispering Jack*, but it is probably fitting to conclude this final chapter by noting that this phenomenon constitutes a development that was structurally significant for the local industry. Possibly for the first time in Australian rock music history, this was an audience built primarily on stadium performances, in what might be regarded as the invention of a local, mainstream, version of arena-rock. That is quite an invention. Throw in a dollop of 'the Australian spirit', delivered by 'the local hero', speaking with 'the voice of the common man', and it is not hard to understand why these concert tours continued to be the headline events Jim Schembri (1994) describes in his report for *The Age* newspaper on a series of concerts Farnham was performing in Melbourne in 1994:

> The last time there was this much fuss about a concert tour in Australia, the Tibetan leader, the Dalai Lama, was in town. But his gigs were free. People pay to see John Farnham. And John Farnham will be doing (at last counting) 10 concerts at the National Tennis Centre. The Dalai Lama only did one.

For Australian audiences in the aftermath of *Whispering Jack* and over more than three decades subsequent to its release, the Dalai Lama would always come a distant second to John Farnham. That's quite a legacy generated by the album we have examined in this book.

Notes

Introduction

1 As we will see in Chapter 3, there are two other primary contenders, both of which are now embedded as advertising jingles: the ABC's signature tune 'We are Australian' and Qantas's appropriation of Peter Allen's 'I Still Call Australia Home'.

2 In addition to the event in 2020 already discussed, it featured significantly in another bushfire benefit concert in 2009, where Farnham shared the stage with Coldplay's Chris Martin to sing 'You're the Voice' (which Martin has said was actually the first song Coldplay learned to play).

Chapter 1

1 A short extract from this interview is among the video material included in the online exhibition dealing with Farnham's career on the Australian National Film and Sound Archive referred to earlier.

2 When ABC TV began broadcasting all night music videos on Friday nights, Saturday mornings and Saturday nights in 1987, they chose *Rage* as the title of the programme.

3 According to the Macquarie Dictionary, the word 'bogan' describes an 'uncouth or unsophisticated person regarded

as being of low social status'. It is of relatively recent
coinage, and is widely used as a term of abuse, but also
in some instances, as a social or class identity to be
celebrated as a mark of resistance to polite, middle-class
culture.

4   I should acknowledge here that Jon Stratton makes a
powerful argument against this view in Chapter 3 of his
Australian Rock (2005), drawing upon the distinctiveness of
the post-punk music scene in Perth as a way of describing a
national sound.

Chapter 2

1   The Fairlight was the first digital synthesizer and sampler. It
was invented by two young Australians, Kim Ryrie and Peter
Vogel, in 1979. The Fairlight got its name from a hydrofoil
(itself named after the Sydney suburb Fairlight) on Sydney
Harbour which Ryrie and Vogel saw passing by as they
worked on their invention in Ryrie's grandmother's Point
Piper garage. In addition to the reproduction of acoustic
instruments, the Fairlight allowed musicians to incorporate
any type of sound into their music: it is credited with
initiating the era of digital sampling.

2   Doug Brady told me that some of the bass sounds that are
such distinctive features of the album were the product of
two different sounds being played live on synthesizers and
mixed as one sound.

3   This is not the only one; many of these reaction blogs
respond to 'You're the Voice' and in similar terms.

Chapter 3

1 This term refers to the manner in which people form emotional attachments to figures with whom they can only interact through the media or by witnessing their performances as fans, rather than through a direct face-to-face personal relationship. While at one time such parasocial interactions were seen as compensatory, plugging gaps in the construction of social community, in more recent years the development of social media and other modes of interacting more directly with public figures has made this kind of relation seem to be a more common and less pathological element of social experience (Turner 2014: 26–9).

2 Ausmusic was launched by Hawke in 1989, and it made a significant contribution to education and training, as well as a 'modest contribution to the export market of Australian services' (Breen: 161).

3 I have personal experience of this, as I was appointed by the newly elected state Labor government in Queensland in 1994 to chair its Arts Advisory Committee, a role which included an explicit brief to find ways to modify existing arts grants programmes in order to incorporate proposals from musicians working in popular music, with the aim of supporting such activities as CD production and regional tours, for instance.

Chapter 4

1 This doesn't have to be positive. In many cases, the ordinariness of the public personality lies in their ability to mess things up; there is enormous media appetite for documenting the ways in which the lives of the modern celebrity are difficult, tormented or dysfunctional. In these cases, their ordinariness makes them seem less than the rest of us, and their exploits are consumed via the media as a form of public schadenfreude.

2   Lisa Edwards built on this exposure to develop a solo career in addition to her work as a backing vocalist, releasing three solo albums so far (the latest in 2021), and reaching the top five in the ARIA singles charts in 1992 with her cover of Godley and Crème's 'Cry'.

References

Adams, C. (2015), 'Australia's Favourite Voice John Farnham Returns . . . Again'. *Herald Sun*, 16 January. Available online: Australia's favourite voice John Farnham returns . . . again | Herald Sun (accessed 27 April 2021).

Adams, C. (2018), 'Why John Farnham Was Nearly "Rock-Blocked" From Recording "You're the Voice"'. *news.com.au*, 11 April. Available online: https://www.news.com.au/entertainment/music/why-john-farnham-was-nearly-rockblocked-from-youre-the-voice/news-story/e048f2d4550a8b4c1a28e2eba4909f6 (accessed 3 March 2021).

Apter, J. (2016a), *Playing to Win: The Definitive Biography of John Farnham*. Carlton: Nero.

Apter, J. (2016b), 'Whispering Jack Turns 30 and Still the Biggest Selling Oz Album Ever'. *Daily Review*, 24 November. Available online: https://dailyreview.com.au/whispering-jack-turns-30-still-biggest-selling-oz-album-ever/ (accessed 1 March 2021).

Baker, G.A. (1986a), 'Australia '86: Global Impact. Novelty Image Wears Off, Paving Way for Super Talent for the '90s'. *Billboard*, 15 November, A4. A22, A23.

Baker, G.A. (1986b), 'John Farnham Returns to Limelight Down Under'. *Billboard*, 27 December, 77, 78.

Baker, G.A. (1988), 'Wheatley Weaves FM Web to Australia'. *Billboard*, 26 March, 58, 61.

Barthes, R. (2010), First published 1981. *The Grain of the Voice: Interviews 1962–1980*. Translated by L. Coverdale. Chicago: Northwestern University Press.

Bennett, T., L. Grossberg, S. Frith, J. Shepherd, and G. Turner (eds). (1993), *Rock and Popular Music: Politics, Policies, Institutions*. London: Routledge.

Billboard (1987), 'Farnham a Hit in Europe: RCA Builds Momentum for Aussie Act'. 16 May, 70.

Boorstin, D. (1971), *The Image: A Guide to Pseudo-Events in America*. New York: Atheneum.

Brabazon, T. (2000), *Tracking the Jack: A Retracing of the Antipodes*. Sydney: UNSW Press.

Brabazon, T. (2005), *Liverpool of the South Seas: Perth and its Popular Music*. Nedlands: UWA Press.

Breen, M. (2006), *Rock Dogs: Politics and the Australian Music Industry*. Lanham, ML: University Press of America. First published Melbourne, Pluto Press 1999.

Canberra Times (1987), 'Farnham Sweeps Board'. 20 July, 1.

Chambers, Iain (1985), *Urban Rhythms: Pop Music and Popular Culture*. London: Macmillan.

Clay, L. (2011), 'Interview with Brett Garsed'. 25 August. Available online: Interview with Brett Garsed - Live4guitar | Online Guitar Community (accessed 10 June 2021).

Commonwealth of Australia (1994), *Creative Nation: Commonwealth Cultural Policy*. Canberra: Department of Communication and the Arts.

Engleheart, M. (2010), *Blood, Sweat and Beers: Oz Rock from the Aztecs to Rose Tattoo*. Sydney: HarperCollins.

Fiske, J., B. Hodge, and G. Turner (1987), *Myths of Oz: Reading Australian Popular Culture*. St Leonards: Allen and Unwin.

Frith, S. (1988), *Music for Pleasure: Essays in the Sociology of Pop*. Cambridge: Polity.

Gazzo, J. (2015), *John Farnham: The Untold Story*. North Sydney: Penguin Random House.

Glendinning, L. (2002), First published 1994. 'You're the Voice and We Understand It'. *Sydney Morning Herald*, 4 December. Available online: https://www.smh.co.au/national/youre-the-voice-and-we-understand-it-20021204-gdfwt6.html (accessed 28 April 2021).

Griffen-Foley, B. (2009), *Changing Stations: The Story of Australian Commercial Radio*. Sydney: UNSW Press.

Grossberg, L. (1984), 'Another Boring Day in Paradise: Rock'n'roll and the Empowerment of Everyday Life'. *Popular Music*, 4: 225–58.

Grossberg, L. (1992), *We Gotta Get Outa This Place: Popular Conservatism and Postmodern Culture*. New York: Routledge.

Gunders, J. (2012), 'Electronic Dance Music, the Rock Myth, and Authenticity'. *Perfect Beat*, 13(7): 147–89.

Hayward, P. (ed.). (1992a), *From Pop to Punk to Postmodernism: Popular Music and Australian Culture from the 1960s to the 1990s*. St Leonards: Allen and Unwin.

Hayward, P. (1992b), 'Introduction: Charting Australian Music, History and Identity'. In P. Hayward (ed.), *From Pop to Punk to Postmodernism: Popular Music and Australian Culture from the 1960s to the 1990s*, 1–8. St Leonards: Allen and Unwin.

Hayward, P. (1992c), 'Sound Commodities: Copyright, Sampling and Cultural Politics'. *Media Information Australia*, 64: 42–7.

Hebdige, D. (1979), *Subculture: The Meaning of Style*. London: Methuen.

Hebdige, D. (1987), *Cut'n'Mix: Culture, Identity and Caribbean Music*. London: Comedia.

Hesmondhalgh, D. and K. Negus (eds). (2002), *Popular Music Studies*. London: Bloomsbury.

Homan, S. (2003), *The Mayor's a Square: Live Music and Law and Order in Sydney*. Newtown: Local Consumption.

Homan, S. (2006a), 'Popular Music'. In S. Cunningham and G. Turner (eds), *The Media and Communications in Australia*, 2nd edn, 238–58. St Leonards: Allen and Unwin.

Homan, S. (2006b), 'Introduction'. In S. Homan (ed.), *Access All Eras: Tribute Bands and Global Pop Culture*, 1–16. Maidenhead: Open University Press.

Homan, S. (2007), 'Classic Hits in a Digital Era: Music Radio and the Australian Music Industry'. *Media International Australia*, 123: 95–108.

Homan, S. (2014), 'Music'. In B. Griffen-Foley (ed.), *A Companion to the Australian Media*, 283–5. Melbourne: Australian Scholarly Publishing.

I Like Your Old Stuff (2017), '1987 – The Greatest Year for Aussie Music Ever?'. 8 October. Available online: www.ilikeyouroldstuff.com/news/1987-the-greatest-year-for-aussie-music-ever (accessed 20 February 2021).

Jamal AKA Jamel (2021), 'REACTION John Farnham "You're The Voice"'. 20 March. Available online: https://www.youtube.com/watch?v=7NOLlgSIAAA (accessed 28 March 2021).

Jonker, E. (1992), 'Contemporary Music and Commercial Radio'. *Media Information Australia*, 64: 24–30.

Kruger, D. (1987), 'John Farnham Reviews'. *Variety*. Available online: https://www.google.com/search?q=reviews+variety+john+farnham+december+9%2C+1987&oq=&aqs=chrome.0.69i59i450l8.80318705j0j15&sourceid=chrome&ie=UTF-8 (accessed 1 March 2021).

Lenhoff, A.S. and D. Robertson (2019), *Classic Keys: Keyboard Sounds That Launched Rock Music*. Denton TX: University of North Texas Press.

Marks, B. (2015), 'The Rise of the Synthesizer: How an Electronics Whiz Kid Gave the 1980s its Signature Sound'. *Collectors Weekly*, 1 October. Available online: https://collectorswe

ekly.com/articles/rise-of-the-synthesizer (accessed 11 April 2021).

Matthison, J. and O. Gunsberg (2021), 'Idle Australians Episode 6. Why Did "You're the Voice" Have Bagpipes? And How Did It End up Being Sung in Greek?'. Available online: https://po dcasts.apple.com/au/podcast/ep-6-why-did-youre-voice -have-bagpipes-how-did-it-end/id1551914016?i=10005202 87793 (accessed 10 May 2021).

McIntyre, P. (2007), 'Copyright and Creativity: Changing Paradigms and the Implications for Intellectual Property and the Music Industry'. *Media International Australia*, 123: 82–94.

Middleton, R. (1990), *Studying Popular Music*. Milton Keynes: Open University Press.

National Film and Sound Archive, 'You're The Voice'. Available online; https://www.nfsa.gov.au/tags/youre-voice (accessed 4 February 2021).

Neal, M. (2021), '1991 Saw the Music Industry Turned Upside Down and, 30 Years Later. Its Echoes Remain'. *ABC News*, 6 March. Available online: https://www.abc.net.au/news/20 21-03-06/how-1991-saw-the-music-industry-turned-upside- down/13148150 (accessed 6 March 2021).

Newman, M. (1989), 'John Farnham's "Voice" Rises from the Past'. *Billboard*, 14 October, 33, 35.

Nichols, D. (2017), *Dig: Australian Rock and Pop 1960–1985*. Melbourne: Verse Chorus Press.

Nimmervoll, E. (2004), *Friday on My Mind: A Year by Year Account of Popular Music in the Australian Charts*. Rowville: Five Mile Press.

Oldham, P. (2013), 'Suck More Piss: How the Confluence of Melbourne-Based Audiences, Musicians and Iconic Scenes Informed the Oz Rock Identity'. *Perfect Beat*, 14(2): 120–39.

Petridis, A. (2019), 'Raves, Robots, and Writhing Bodies: How Electronic Music Rewired the World'. *The Guardian*, 15 March.

Available online: Raves, robots and writhing bodies: how electronic music rewired the world | Electronic music | The Guardian (accessed 15 April, 2021).

Potts, J. (1992), 'Heritage Rock: Pop Music on Australian Radio'. In P. Hayward (ed.), *From Pop to Punk to Postmodernism: Popular Music and Australian Culture from the 1960s to the 1990s*, 55–67. St Leonards: Allen and Unwin.

Schembri, J. (1994), 'The Rise and Rise of John 'Voice' Farnham'. *The Age*, 11 March, 3.

Shepherd, J. (1991), *Music as Social Text*. Cambridge: Polity.

Shepherd, J. and P. Wicke (1997), *Music and Cultural Theory*. Cambridge: Polity.

Shuker, R. (1993), *Understanding Popular Music*. London: Routledge.

Stratton, J. (2007), *Australian Rock. Essays on Popular Music*. Perth: API Network Books.

Stratton, J. and J. Dale with T. Mitchell (eds). (2020), *An Anthology of Australian Albums*. New York: Bloomsbury.

Sutton, P. (1986), 'Farnham is "the voice": Whispering Jack no Phantom'. *Canberra Times: Good Times*, 21 November, 9.

Sutton, P. (1987), 'Solid Gold Launch for First Australian Disc'. *Canberra Times*, 22 May, 6.

Tripp, P. (1987), 'Farnham Concerts are Lensed: Called Biggest Production Down Under'. *Billboard*, 4 April, 62.

Turner, G. (1989), 'Rock Music, National Culture and Cultural Policy'. In T. Bennett (ed.), *Rock Music: Politics and Policy*, 1–7, Griffith University: Institute for Cultural Policy Studies.

Turner, G. (1992), 'Australian Popular Music and its Contexts'. In P. Hayward (ed.), *From Pop to Punk to Postmodernism: Popular Music and Australian Culture from the 1960s to the 1990s*, 11–24. St Leonards: Allen and Unwin.

Turner, G. (1993), 'Who Killed the Radio Star: The Death of Teen Radio in Australia'. In T. Bennett, S. Frith, L. Grossberg, J.

Shepherd, and G. Turner (eds), *Rock and Popular Music: Politics, Policies, Institutions*, 141–54. London: Routledge.

Turner, G. (1994), *Making it National: Nationalism and Australian Popular Culture*. St Leonards: Allen and Unwin.

Turner, G. (2014), *Understanding Celebrity*, 2nd edn. London: Sage.

Variety (1987), 'Farnham, Crowded House Sweep Majority of Aussie Music Prizes'. 22 July, 77.

Walker, C.J. (2005), *Inner City Sound: Punk and Post-Punk in Australia, 1976–1985*. Melbourne: Verse Chorus Press. First edition 1982, Sydney: Wild and Woolley Press.

Walker, C.J., T. Hogan, and P. Beilharz (2012), 'Rock 'n' Labels: Tracking the Australian Recording Industry in "The Vinyl Age": Part Two: 1970–1995, and after'. *Thesis Eleven*, 110(1): 112–31.

Watterson, R. (1989), 'The Role of Commercial Radio in the Development of Australian Rock Music'. In T. Bennett (ed.), *Rock Music: Politics and Policy*, 7–13. Griffith University: Institute for Cultural Policy Studies.

Zion, L. (1988), 'The Sound of Australian Music'. In V. Burgmann and J. Lee (eds), *Constructing a Culture*, 209–22. Melbourne: Penguin.

Zuel, B. (2000), 'The Battle for the Nation's Soul'. *Sydney Morning Herald*, 30 November, 20.

Zuel, B. (2016), 'Wind Back Wednesday'. 22 November. Available online: https//www.bernardzuel.nbet/post2016/16/11/23/wind-back-Wednesday (accessed 19 February 2021).

Discography

Farnham, John (1980), *Uncovered*. Wheatley: Sony BMG.

Farnham, John (1986), *Whispering Jack*. Wheatley: Sony BMG, RCA.

Farnham, John (1988), *Age of Reason*. Sony BMG.

Farnham, John (1990), *Chain Reaction*. Wheatley: Sony BMG, RCA.

Farnham, John (1996), *Romeo's Heart*. Gotham: Sony BMG, RCA.

Farnham, John (1997), *33 1/3*. Gotham: Sony BMG, RCA.

Farnham, John (1997), *Anthology 1*. Gotham: Sony BMG, RCA.

Farnham, John and Olivia Newton-John (2015), *John Farnham and Olivia Newton-John: Highlights from Two Strong Hearts Live*. Sony.

Little River Band (1984), *Playing to Win*. Capitol.

Tears for Fears (1984), *Songs from the Big Chair*. Phonogram.

Yes (1983), *90125*. Atco.

Personal interviews

Brady, Doug 30 April, 2021.

Fraser, Ross 19 May, 2021.

Hirschfelder, David 5 April, 2021.

Index

www.ingramcontent.com/pod-product-compliance
Ingram Content Group UK Ltd.
Pitfield, Milton Keynes, MK11 3LW, UK
UKHW022246060726
473012UK00003B/53